Best wishes
Neil

Harry Titley.

A Staffordshire Lad

Reflections of Wartime Youth

Harry Titley

authorHOUSE®

AuthorHouse™ UK Ltd.
500 Avebury Boulevard
Central Milton Keynes, MK9 2BE
www.authorhouse.co.uk
Phone: 08001974150

© 2009 Harry Titley. All rights reserved.

No part of this book may be reproduced, stored in a retrieval system, or transmitted by any means without the written permission of the author.

First published by AuthorHouse 4/21/2009

ISBN: 978-1-4389-4179-0 (sc)

Printed in the United States of America
Bloomington, Indiana

This book is printed on acid-free paper.

Dedication

To Ann, my dear wife, whose support and patience have been invaluable.

And to Julie, my dear daughter, who came up with the idea,

And to my two grandchildren, Tom and Annie, who I like to think will read it sometime.

Acknowledgements

I am indebted to a number of people who supplied information, photographs and shared memories and I apologise to anyone I have not included.

I am grateful for the help given by John Abberley from The Sentinel, the staff of the Apedale Heritage Centre, my cousin Doreen Hancock, my old friend, Phil Harrison, my sister Joan Martyn, my son-in-law Steve Gullick for his invaluable help with the processing and preparation of the photographs, Colonel Klaus Trares, Luftwaffenunterstutzungsgruppe - Koln-Wahn and Kathryn Ing, Leycett On-line.

For research and assistance with archive material and advice, I am grateful to the staff, and particularly Paul Smith, of the Newcastle-Under-Lyme Public Library Information Department.

I am grateful for permission to use information from reports on mining disasters in North Staffordshire from Keele University.

I am grateful to the staff of the former Orme Boys and Hassell Street schools for their assistance and permission to use photographs and information.

For permission to use information and photographs associated with Newcastle-under-Lyme School, I am grateful to Ian Cartwright.

Although I didn't use any material from the book Images of England – Newcastle-Under-Lyme-School by Caroline

Davis, much of the information confirmed my own research and I am grateful for it.

I am especially grateful to my wife Ann who, without her commercial experience, proof-reading and patience, I never would have completed the book.

The poem Dear Brown Bread is by A P Herbert

I am grateful to A M Heath & Company Ltd for permission to use the poem and quote by Barbara Euphan Todd from her book Worzel Gummige.

The poem and quote from Gunga Din by Rudyard Kipling.

The quote from Modern Manners by P J O'Rourke.

The poem by E F A Geach from Oxford that I first read in Nevil Shute's autobiography Slide Rule.

The report on The Diglake Disaster is a contemporary account of the incident.

Every effort has been made to contact all copyright holders and, through my publishers, I will ensure any errors or omissions brought to their attention, will be made good in any future editions.

'I'd been watching some ragged rooks float down like a bundle of tattered, black rags before settling on a group of mature oaks across the lane in Finney Green; a prelude to dark and sinister invaders from a foreign soil. They were calling to each other peevishly as if they too wished to be out of sight from the menaces of the night.'

TABLE OF CONTENTS

Introduction — xiii

CHAPTER ONE
Arriving — 1

CHAPTER TWO
Gardening — 5

CHAPTER THREE
Developing — 9

CHAPTER FOUR
Visiting — 17

CHAPTER FIVE
Rationing — 27

CHAPTER SIX
Mining — 44

CHAPTER SEVEN
Learning - Rye Croft School — 55

CHAPTER EIGHT
Learning - Hassell Street School — 58

CHAPTER NINE
Playing — 69

CHAPTER TEN
Walking — 83

CHAPTER ELEVEN
Holidaying   89

CHAPTER TWELVE
Learning - Orme Boys School   115

CHAPTER THIRTEEN
Earning   125

CHAPTER FOURTEEN
Biking   136

CHAPTER FIFTEEN
Learning - Newcastle High School   141

CHAPTER SIXTEEN
Flitting   160

CHAPTER SEVENTEEN
Flying   166

CHAPTER EIGHTEEN
Serving   171

CHAPTER NINETEEN
Re-visiting   215

Epilogue   218

Those That Touched My Early Life   219

About the Author   222

Nunquam non Nova

Not new things but in a new way

The motto of Newcastle (Staffordshire) High School

INTRODUCTION

When mists dissolve on a winter's morn,
The clarity of the scene's re-born,
As memory, renewed by sound or smell
Re-kindles times of yore as well
To share with oneself a childhood stage,
Long forgotten for many an age,
And when into the mist it wanes,
Only sadness, a kind of grief, remains.

I have been amazed how memories of my childhood have stayed with me so vividly throughout my life; especially now that I find it so difficult to recall even recent events. However, the perspective of the years helped to give me a more comprehensive clarity to my early life. As a 'recall exercise', writing these reflections of my youth has been both invaluable and revealing. It has opened the gates to my past life. I have been surprised at the memories that have been locked away for so many years. I have awakened a thousand latent joys and half-forgotten sorrows. It's as though my memory as reconstructed my early life with a clarity that has astounded me both in the visual and the psychological sense. Memory is such a powerful alchemist. It seems to me that memory is like a street guide with many cul-de-sacs barred to access, and I have learnt that perseverance, patience and concentration can provide the code to unlock many of them, or find another way round. Remembering incidents of years ago has rekindled the emotions experienced at the time. I've laughed, cried, become angry, elated, embarrassed and sad. As I have become older, I have realised that age is retrospective.

It has also been an interesting exercise visiting and re-visiting those places, which have been associated with our lives. My wife, Ann, and I have been able to share locations important to us before and since we met. And as the pith drains away from my old bones, I now have the narrative to reflect upon.

I have written some parts reflectively and some retrospectively, so ignoring the traditional rules of tense. Sometimes I would type away in 'diary fashion' adding bits and pieces as they came to me, but more often than not I would get lost in the past and re-live the times as if they were happening for the first time.

I thought it useful to provide profiles of my parents and grandparents so as to give an insight into my beginnings, and also to provide a comparison of the impact and disciplines of family life as it was then to what it has become today. I was sixty-four when I started to write this account and at that age the memory tends to fade somewhat. Memories can play tricks and what one may have thought fact has been what one has been told, hints, half-truths or family myths. However, I have tried very hard to discriminate between the two and feel that I have succeeded to a large degree. Where I may have failed is with the accuracy of a few of the dates and a couple of surnames for which I apologise and hope it won't distract too much from the real issues.

W H Titley

CHAPTER ONE

ARRIVING

• 1 •

The young mother, utterly drained from a difficult pregnancy and confinement, and with this her third child in four years, watched in horror, helplessly, from her bed as the nurse suspended her baby from the first floor window. Her small black Ford was parked in the road and a young girl waved her congratulations from an open passenger window. The mother, looking more than her twenty-eight years, pleaded mutely and desperately for her baby. Her black hair, damp with perspiration, stuck to her forehead and her large brown eyes filled with tears of dread for her new-born child.

The midwife's small black bag, containing the gruesome tools of her trade, sat open on a cane chair beside the bed. The aftermath of the birth lay in a disorderly mess on the floor. The hot soapy water in the white enamel bucket still steamed as it adjusted to the ambient temperature of the room. The pile of unused newspapers, gathered over weeks for the purpose, sat in the corner whilst the rest lay screwed

A Staffordshire Lad

up on the floor half-hiding the gory remnants of the afterbirth.

It is Monday the sixth of July 1936, and although only eight o'clock, the warmth from the morning sun, risen just three hours earlier, is gathering strength. The bees are busily collecting nectar and dispersing pollen amongst the well-laid out borders below, ablaze with a mass of red double-headed Geraniums. A low hawthorn hedge separates a rough unmade road from four fields. A winding brook cuts them centrally and deeply before disappearing into a tunnel under the embankment of a railway. The twin track, high above the fields, creates a barrier screening the allotments and terraced housing beyond. All that is left of the 7.50 L.M.S. steam engine from Silverdale hauling its three brown coaches full of workers and schoolchildren around the long curve before slowing down into Newcastle station, are a few puffs of rapidly disappearing smoke, and its penetrating whistle as it passes through the level crossing at the Brampton.

I am born.

The daily paper, delivered just half an hour before me, includes a statement that the L.M.S. has announced its summer fares. For a two shillings' package, a passenger's luggage can be collected in advance and delivered to the final destination for the owner's arrival. The cost of a monthly return ticket is one penny per mile, or one and a half pennies per mile first class.

The 'entertainments' page advertises that Fay Compton and Owen Nares are appearing in the comedy "Call It A Day" at The Globe; John Geilgud, Edith Evans and Peggy Ashcroft are in Chekhov's "The Seagull" at The New Theatre, and at St. Martin's, Rex Harrison is one of the stars of the comedy " Heroes Don't Care."

The inside front page is full of the growing threat of Hitler's Nazi war machine in Germany.

And later that day, on the front page of the final edition of the Evening Sentinel, there are reports of the visit of Dame Elizabeth Cadbury opening the Westlands sports ground; the trial of a murdered woman at Tipton; the vandalism of a shop window in Newcastle by two youths; a declaration by the transport ministry that it is to take over trunk roads to solve the problems of modern traffic requirements, and a case involving breach of promise. All are overshadowed by the news from Germany and the hectic activity of strained diplomatic relations in a world still desperately trying to come to terms with the terrible effects of the Great War just eighteen years previously.

• 2 •

My birthplace is number thirty Albemarle Road in Cross Heath, a northern district of Newcastle-under-Lyme in the county of Staffordshire.

On 11 August 1936 I am christened at St George's church Newcastle with eight other children. They are Sidney Dudley Barber, Margaret Myatt, Elaine Oakley, Beryl Dale, Patricia Ann Lawton, May Challinor, Joan Finney and Mary Hughes. Uncle Harry, my intended godfather has been delayed, so Uncle George substitutes.

Initially Albemarle Road consisted of only eighteen houses, evenly numbered from two to thirty six and built just after the First World War. Later it was extended to a junction with Lower Milehouse Lane. The estate includes Charter Road with branches to King Street and Poplar Avenue. This new estate was built to house the inhabitants of Lower Street, Fletcher Street, and Goose Street that were demolished for the provision of a new road. In this area lived some of the poorest people in Newcastle. A report on public health described it as 'seats of excessive mortality' ... and, 'the habits of the people residing in these parts are not as good as they should be'.

My home is a typical council house of the period, the end of a row of four. All have wooden gates and picket fences marking the boundary between the gardens and the unmade footpaths. Although most of the houses in the block, which includes Orton Road and part of Hassam Avenue, are council, a number are privately owned, or privately rented, as is ours. The owner is a Mr Lockett from Keele who collects the rent of five shillings a week each month. There is a small front garden, which is joined to a large rear garden by a path at the side of house alongside another narrow stretch of lawn. It's always immaculate. Dad is a good gardener. Whenever he is asked how he manages to grow such healthy plants, he says, "I always give 'em a good feed of Sok."

CHAPTER TWO

GARDENING

• 1 •

Sok! I've never heard the word since, but like the liquid fertilizer it described, I guess it was Dad's own invention. Dad was never so at peace as he was in his garden. He was as good a gardener as he was a grocer, and he was a very good grocer. Everyone that knew him agreed that his undoubted skills in the shop matched those that he had in the garden. When he was in the shop he looked like one imagined a grocer to look like and somehow managed to transform himself to look like a gardener when he was in the garden.

He was shaped like a Spanish onion. His face was as round as an apple and his cheeks were as rosy as two peaches. He had large, twinkling eyes as blue as Lavender. Indeed, he was a very good advertisement for the two main activities in his life.

Thursday afternoons were his half-days off. After dinner he'd have an hour with the Daily Herald. That is, he would read it for half an hour and sleep under it for the rest to emerge damp and pink and ready for the day. Regardless of the season, he'd put on a pair of well-worn 'wellies', an old tweed jacket and a sad-looking velour trilby hat and then he'd light up his old briar selected from a rack at the back of the outhouse door, and, swathed in clouds of blue smoke, he'd toddle up the uneven red-brick path to the shed at the top of the garden.

Dad always knew exactly what he was going to do. He'd had a week to think about it. His steady pace belied his work output. Paradoxically, he could achieve more than some working twice as hard. The shed was an Aladdin's cave of homemade garden aids and hand-me-down tools each having its own unique place and he knew them all. There were dibbers made from the stale of an old rake, an ancient riddle, balls of string, skeins of raffia, piles of Hessian sacks, an old brass hand-pumped fly-kill spray that squirted his special brew of soapy water, old tins as rusty as the nails and screws they contained, fruit boxes of the type that had pegs in the corners to support the box above; ideal to rest the sheets of glass that he used to 'bring on' the early seedlings. The battered old shed had a pleasant, earthy smell that always reminded me of autumn. A misshapen old whetstone balanced on the top of a pile of 'Staffordshire Blue' house bricks was hidden at the back of the shed. Dad's first job was to sharpen his penknife. He'd dribble a spot of water from the rain tub onto the stone and, with a technique developed over many years, he'd put a fine edge to the blade. Finally, he'd strop it on the palm of his hand for a minute or so.

Predominantly, he grew flowers, but there was always a small corner for the odd salad and small vegetable plants to help out the family budget. He had a patch for cut flowers such as Sweet Williams, Asters and Carnations, but his main interest was in Geraniums. What he didn't know about the cultivation of Geraniums wasn't worth knowing. There seemed to be an indefinable affinity between Dad and his Geraniums. Initially, from just a packet of seeds, his summer borders were constantly ablaze with the glorious, red double blooms of his favourite plant nurtured with ample helpings of his homemade 'Sok'.

Passing folk would stop and lean on the fence to admire the results of his industry. On Sunday mornings some would call in on their way to the cemetery to buy a bunch of cut flowers. Dad was a man of few words, but he would share with them his reflections on the weather, the condition of the soil, or the current problems of garden pests.

He fervently believed in 'all things natural', and especially in putting back into the ground what was constantly being taken out of it. He'd gather buckets of manure from the four fields and stack it at the back of the shed until it was well rotted down. He saved the soot from his chimney in the same place. 'Sok' was a mixture of the old manure, rainwater and one or two undisclosed organic additives, all put together in a rusty oil drum at the top of the garden. Like an old witch weaving her magic spells over her cauldron, he never passed it without giving it a couple of good stirs with an old stair rod and a few whispered words of encouragement.

In August he'd break off the tender green side shoots of the Geraniums and bob them into the ground in the shelter of the mother plants. He always said August was the best month for taking cuttings. Then towards the end of September, before the first frost, he'd dust down his antique collection of assorted clay pots and transplant the young plants and a few of his stock plants ready for moving indoors for the winter.

In the absence of a greenhouse, he had to make do with the windowsills inside the house. Every window was filled with Geraniums and the pots sat on a vast assortment of old, crazed saucers, dishes and rusty fruit tin lids that he'd rescued from one place or another. Mum accepted the situation philosophically. After all, Dad cleaned the windows and kept the sills tidy. And so he did, and more. Religiously, every Sunday morning, he checked the health of every plant and the moisture content of the soil before pinching out any young buds and dead leaves.

As the days grew warmer he'd take the Geraniums out into the yard for a bit of an airing to 'harden them off', and bring them all in again before the evening grew too cool. And after the last frost, when late spring merged into early summer, the borders would once again be filled with his precious plants.

• 2 •

Dad is a really good gardener. It's his main hobby and a credit to him. In the summer the lawns are edged with annual flowerbeds and roses bought from Dobbie's seed catalogues. In the winter he plants wallflowers, or 'gillivers' as he calls them, meaning gillyflowers, for the following year.

If Geraniums are his first love, then roses run a close second. He has bush and shrub, but most prominent are ramblers and climbers. He built sections of rustic trellis to separate different sections of the garden. The one by the house is covered with American Pillar and Seven Sisters. He sprays them regularly to protect them from aphids, mildew and black spot. The garden is an oasis surrounded by our neighbours' vegetable patches and unkempt stretches of grass.

I'm proud that we have the nicest garden on the block.

CHAPTER THREE

DEVELOPING

• 1 •

Conversely, the only time Mum ever goes into the garden is on Mondays to hang out the washing. There are unambiguous demarcation lines between Mum's and Dad's individual territories, and clear divisions between what they each consider to be their duties and responsibilities. Whilst Dad's stature is small and accentuated by his rotundity, Mum is tall, about five feet seven, with thick dark hair and large brown eyes. I see her now with her head slightly tending towards her left shoulder, her big brown eyes, warm and shining, and her open face smiling and contented. Yes, most contented – a person of simple needs, devoted to raising her family through difficult times with very little income. She has a quiet, mild disposition. She never loses her temper, or raises her voice. She is a kind, considerate and loving mother. Like many women of her generation, she has no hobbies. She doesn't sew or knit; she just darns the socks and sews on the buttons. She doesn't read in any great depth. The only times she relaxes, and is separated from her flock, wrap over apron, is with her weekly magazine 'The Home Companion'.

As a young girl, Mum and her two sisters were heavily involved in running Ivy Cottage, the family home. After leaving school at fourteen, they went into service, although Mum worked for a short spell in the Newcastle workhouse, the buildings of which now form part of the City General (University Hospital of North Staffordshire). Her two elder sisters, Beattie and Ruth, went into service in Manchester, and later, Mum went to Keele about a mile away from her home in Madeley Heath.

For young girls from working class families there was rarely any alternative to 'going into service' when they left school. Parents just couldn't afford to keep them and many of those providing places took full advantage of the situation. The girls were little more than skivvies having to work long hours on mundane chores for very little pay and with few breaks to visit home, or to enjoy themselves. They spent their teenage years in a continual round of menial scrubbing, cleaning and household drudgery, missing out on what should have been the happiest years of their lives.

Mum was more fortunate than most. She served with Mr and Mrs Gregory who'd been missionaries in India. Her main responsibility was nursemaid to their two daughters. The Gregory's were kind-hearted folk who took Mum into their family circle, but it was still very hard work with long hours and only one day off every two weeks. However, Mum held them in high esteem and remembered them with fondness having the two girls for bridesmaids at her wedding.

• 2 •

We are a poor family in that we have barely sufficient income to match our outgoings, but this is compensated for by Mum's sound discipline in handling the money. Poverty has certain relativism. We never go hungry. We are always well dressed, kept warm and clean and well cared for. We are nursed, healed and cured from accident and illness. As a measure of these standards, we are rich indeed.

And because there is so little variance in the circumstances of our neighbours, there is no envy or petty jealousies. I feel totally insulated, comfortable, safe and loved. It is in this atmosphere of happy contentment that I move from babyhood to an independent, free-spirited and carefree childhood. Although content just to be with Mum, I have an inherent craving always to be out of doors.

I am three years old. The transmission from inside to outside brings with it an early realisation that there is an acute difference between boys and girls, and it isn't just that girls sit on the lavatory and sing, and boys stand up in front of it and whistle, or that boys have short haircuts and girls have plaits, or even that boys wear short trousers and girls long skirts. But also, that boys are habitually hungry and eat almost anything, and that girls are not all sugar and spice, and can dish out physical violence just as much as boys and, what's more, enjoy doing it.

Bernard Burns lives next door but one and is the same age as me. He has curly, brown hair, a perpetual runny nose and eats worms with gusto; the bigger and fatter the better. He holds them head high, covered in black dirt and looks at them approvingly before sucking them into his mouth and devouring them with relish. This is his main objective in life and I admire him for it, mainly because it's something I can't bring myself to do. We spend many happy hours digging up the footpath in front of our house with our steel spades and buckets just to feed Bernard's grisly habit.

Jean Simpkin lives round the corner in Orton Road. She carries with her, her own sense of amusement. And buckets and spades are top of her list of playthings. There we go marching up and down, buckets on heads, and spades on shoulders like two little tin soldiers, stopping occasionally to smack each other's bucket soldierly and smartly with the back of the spade. Jean gets carried away; once started, she can't stop, even when I take my bucket off! Seeing me in pain sparks her off. She clenches her fists, screws up her eyes, screams with excitement and jumps up and down epileptically, her short plaits flying in all directions.

Jean is taller than me. It takes me twelve years to catch up. She takes after her mother, a tall, straight-laced, haughty woman who has the misfortune to have inherited a permanent expression of disapproval from her own mother, Mrs Gumley, who lives with them. The same resemblance can be recognised in Mitzi, their brown and white cocker spaniel, the most unsociable of dogs. Mrs Simpkin focus's me with the end of her nose as though finding it difficult to believe what she apparently doesn't want to see. An image indelibly printed on my mind, almost as though she had bitten into it and left her impression for time immemorial.

Jean is also the same age, but unlike Bernard, whose family flits when he's four, we are destined to go to the same infants and junior schools. We are not compatible, maybe because I am more of a 'Just William' and she is most definitely a 'Violet Elizabeth Bott'.

Bernard's going brings a significant change to my young life. As the Burns' moved out, the Roberts' move in. They have one son, Graham, who is the same age as me. We've already made our acquaintance. We often play together when he visits his grandparents, the Allmans, who are our next door neighbours. We both have the same red pedal cars, which we race and crash and cry in. It's the start of a friendship that will last for all our growing up years.

• 3 •

Inevitably, there are times when I have to be inside. Mum sings all the latest songs to me occasionally joining in with the records on the wireless, although rationing its use because the charge in the accumulator barely lasts the week. Sitting in the window with a green china dog, I count the railway carriages and trucks. As well as passenger trains, a regular number of freight trains haul their thirty-six rattling, empty coal trucks and tender round the sharp bend, the massive wheels grinding the plates, the inside buffers fully depressed, as the engines steam on the single track branch line to the Brymbo Pit, and then come back full of freshly mined coal about three hours later. On dark winter days, the flickering, ruddy glow of the fire reflects on the faces of the engine driver and fireman. The snorting, iron monsters spray hot ash onto the track and smoke and steam in the air, so like the dragon in my 'Bobby Bear' annual. I want to be an engine driver.

All sorts of vehicles interest me. Whilst our milk is delivered in a van by Bill Massey from Drayton Street in Pool Dam, and in milk bottles, it is closely followed by the Co-op milk cart pulled by an old dray horse. The cart has an open-fronted cab for the milkman, who scoops the milk out of a churn with a gill can and pours it straight into customers' jugs. The horse inevitably stops at the same places through habit. At the corner of Orton Road, the milkman gives the

A Staffordshire Lad

horse its nosebag and two stops later, the old horse lifts its tail and does the necessary, a signal for local housewives to dash out with buckets and shovels, gather it up and scatter it round their roses. There is competition for it. Swettenhams' brightly coloured vans with a large eye above the cab come a number of times during the week to deliver bread and cakes, and on Fridays to bring the weekly orders of groceries. Coalmen, as black as their coal, with black caps and long leather collars attached, and leather, studded strips on their backs, creak and groan only half as much as their long suffering lorry. And because our coalhouse is inside the house, everything in the kitchen has to be covered up and then cleaned thoroughly after each delivery.

The 'electric' and gas are coin-metered. Meters are emptied and shillings stacked into piles of twenty, more money than I've ever seen. About a third of the shillings are given back and the rest are put into small blue bags and stashed away in brown leather pouches.

'Rag Bone!' Every few weeks the rag and bone man trundles passed on his tired old cart pulled by a moth-eaten old nag. Sometimes he has bundles of give-aways in exchange for old clothes. They range from paper windmills to day-old chicks.

In hot summer days Scruffy Sumnall arrives with his bucket of ice cream on the back of a cart pulled by a moth-eaten pony, both on their last legs. The ice cream is yellow and lumpy and Mum won't let us have any because, she tells us, she's seen his nose dripping into it.

Each year the knife-sharpener arrives on his bike which has a stand that lifts the rear wheel off the ground. A belt is attached to pulley wheels on the rear sprocket and grindstone. He has to pedal furiously to maintain sufficient speed to sharpen the knives on the stone.

Around the same time the gypsy woman arrives with a bundle of wooden clothes pegs shaped like armless dolls. Mum always has a few and gives her one of the silver three-penny bits she has been saving for our Christmas stockings.

And so the days and weeks unfold. Mondays are washdays for, it seems to me, the entire neighbourhood. The women race to get the first line full of washing out. There is also zealous rivalry for who has the whitest whites. Collars are scrubbed and whites put in to the boiler with a dolly blue bag. The rest go into the dolly tub, then mangled and put out to dry. The smell of freshly washed, wet linen fills the house. Mum is justifiably proud of her washing. As well as Dad's white shirts and starched collars, there are his white coats and aprons that he wears in the shop. Mondays mean steamy kitchens, clothes maids round the fire, and Sunday roast leftovers hastily served cold or cut up and made into lobby.

Whilst Mondays are washdays, Tuesdays are for ironing. The kitchen table covered with a blanket and an old sheet; flat irons heated on the gas stove and tested for correct temperature on a large piece of green Fairy soap; a basin of cold water to dampen the clothes, later replaced by a sauce bottle with a slot cut in the cork.

Once a week the flues are raked out from the sitting room fireplace. The fire heats the water from a back boiler and also a side oven and a warming box above. The oven is used to make puddings and egg custards, and the warming oven for drying sticks for kindling. Bricks are kept in the oven. These are wrapped in old woollens and used to warm our beds on cold nights. When the weather is really severe, the beds are warmed with the oven shelf wrapped in newspaper. Cleaning the flues is a mucky job and there are a variety of scrapers to get round all the corners. The grate is then black-leaded.

At least every other week Mum takes me to Ivy Cottage to see Aunty Beattie and Granddad Sam. It's my favourite place. We walk from home to Newcastle and catch the Crosville bus to Madeley Heath, about a twenty minutes trip. At Ivy Cottage I am left free to roam.

CHAPTER FOUR

VISITING

• 1 •

Ivy Cottage was Mum's family home. It had been built on the side of Weaver's farm in the middle of the eighteenth century, probably as an extension to the farm, or for a farm labourer, a single man's homestead, or perhaps, at a squeeze, a starter home for a newly wedded couple. Yet this tiny house became home to a family of nine; the rough stone walls infused with the lives and living of a hard working miner, his constantly pregnant wife and seven of their surviving children.

The small building clings on grimly to the farm as if fearful it might slip into the deep railway cutting on its other side. In spite of its size, it is homely, snug, cosy and welcoming. It has a lived-in, friendly personality all of its own. Sparsely furnished with two small rooms downstairs and a single bedroom above, lit by oil lamps, and a single water supply in the back yard. The front door opens onto the living room with a table and four chairs, an old armchair, a sofa and a piano. A black range provides the only source of heat, hot water and means of cooking. Slurry from the cowshed and blood from the slaughterhouse next door seeps over the front door step. A couple of sticky fly-papers hang from the meat hooks on the beam. The small parlour gives access to the stairs. At the top of the stairs are a large landing and a bedroom, the only sleeping accommodation. To the rear of the living room is a small pantry on the left and storage space on the right. The single-track railway that runs by the side of the house serves to bring the coal from Leycett Pit to the coal wharf opposite, and to Madeley station about one mile further south.

I loved everything about Ivy Cottage. I still do. It is part of me. I am part of it. It is a part of what has shaped me. Yet it exists only in my mind and being, but it is real. Even now, I make an annual pilgrimage to it. A ramshackle shed marks its location, but all I see is the tiny house with four windows and a central door overhung with a white rambler rose. I am there now. I see the latch lift and the door opens slowly. A tall, silver-haired old man steps out, picks a half-opened rose and threads it through the buttonhole in the lapel of his jacket with his poor hands, the size of pit shovels, ravaged by sixty years of labour in the pit, scorched and bleeding by intense heat from stoking the boilers in the 'fire hole' to make steam for the engines above. His jacket is black, brushed to death and shiny at the cuff. His waistcoat similarly worn, bedecked with a silver chain hung with medals. A tie, always a tie. The trousers, also dark, yet smart, the hems reflected in a pair of enormous, shiny toe-capped boots. The benign smile, half hidden by a Cupid's bow moustache stained with tobacco, and blue twinkling, expressive eyes suggesting a sensitive and compassionate spirit; proud yet with humility. Retiring though self-assured, emotional but in control. He suits the house. The house suits him. Samuel Tomkinson, my grandfather, born in 1876 at The Bogs Cottage, Keele where he lived with his parents Samuel and Ann, brothers Ernest and Harry, and sisters Virginia, Matilda, Jane, Lucy, Rosetta, Sarah, Dinah and Elizabeth.

To his right, just through the small Georgian window, on an armchair by the fireside, sits an old lady nursing her latest grandchild. It's the last she will ever hold. Named after her own second born, William Harry. Her once dark hair, now white with age and caring, is coiled into a bun and held with a large pin. She's wearing a long-collared white shirt and a blue, white-spotted scarf knotted at the throat, a grey, collarless woollen cardigan with a handkerchief under the left cuff. Her long, grey skirt, lightened through over use and over washing, lifts slightly as she rocks the baby and barely reveals the wrinkled density of her black stockings and the hem of her buckram petticoat. In her right hand is the large back door key on an enormous ring, kept handy to jingle should the baby disturb. Her arms and bosom create a natural cradle for the child, wrought from a lifetime of motherhood. She is content but reflective.

Lucy Lowe, four years older than her tall, handsome, auburn haired husband Sam, was born in 1872 at Black Brook where she lived with her parents Abraham and Susannah, and her siblings William, Henry, Samuel, Matilda, Ruth and Hannah. Her first born was a son, Reginald. As she sits there all alone, but for the sleeping child, she muses over her life and in particular her motherhood; a life that revolved around her family; the fears for Sam in the pit; for herself in childbirth; for her children through illness and accident. And later, for her four sons when they went to war; the girls when they went into service; the relief and pleasure when they came home. Reg, such a bonny, chuckling, cherubic, round faced boy. She remembers him sitting on the wall in the back yard chatting to the engine driver whilst the labourers in the

A Staffordshire Lad

wharf shovel out the coal from the wagons. She smiles as she recalls his urgent entreaty to join the 'railway' at Crewe when he leaves school. But the smile quickly evaporates as she brings to mind the scene when he is just seventeen, waving goodbye to her, his experienced stride coping easily with the sleepers on the line as he made his way to Madeley station and ultimately to the trenches in Northern France.

Almost subconsciously she wipes a tear from her cheek with the back of her hand and, once again, gently rocks the baby Harry on her lap. Harry. Her second son, born just thirteen months after Reg; a joy of a boy. Everything a mother desired in a son. Strong and handsome; independent and free spirited; mischievous and fun-loving, yet responsible and reliable; caring and loving. She harks back to his truancies, his excuses and his hardly believable stories; his desperation to leave school and to be grown up; the arguments with the Head Groomsman at the big house where he first went to work; the wild-eyed steed that lashed out whenever Harry came within range, and the marks of the pikle on its rump that Harry made to remind it of who was boss. Her amusement is substituted with horror when she recalls the telegram from the War Office informing her that 'Private W H Tomkinson is being detained at Dover until confirmation of his age is forthcoming'. He was only sixteen years old and was sent home only to sign up just nine months later and follow his elder brother to France. The fire settles in the grate. The kettle murmurs. The child gurgles. She jingles the key. Albert, born on 31st July 1899, was the most serious of her three sons. His sandy hair suggested a short temper - she knew she needed to watch that. Thoughtful, intelligent, sometimes secretive, he grew up in the shadow of his elder brothers. He followed Reg and Harry into the army, and then joined the railway, first at Stoke and then at Crewe.

Wilf, heralding the new century, was the last of the boys. Her four sons were born in less than five years. Wilf, so handsome, tall and athletic, the apple of every young girl's eye. The trail of broken hearts – not least his mother's as she remembers their heart-breaking goodbye and how she prayed that the war would end before he became another sad statistic. And her own Sam queuing up at the recruiting office, consumed with disappointment when he was told, 'sorry mate, you're too old'.

Lucy is visibly sobbing as she reflects on the most tragic phase of her life. The first six years of the new century bring a period of heartrending and unbearable sadness into the normally happy, fun-filled home. She conceives no less than six times. All but the last either miscarriages or stillborn. She agonises and wrings her hands as she re-lives the pain and torn emotions. She can still hear from her room of confinement above, the fires being made up to cremate the lifeless little bodies. And it is before this same fire that she sees her first daughter, Ilene May, just a toddler, scalded to death when she pulls the large kettle of boiling water on top of her. Within these few years three more daughters are born, Beatrice Mary, Ruth, and her last, Dorothy, the mother of the child on her lap. She is grateful for the survival of her seven children, all of them now grown up, married and most with families of their own. She is proud of her twelve grandchildren and is unaware that she will not live to see another four. Within a few months she pays a heavy toll for her prolific child birth. She sustains a number of strokes and dies distressfully.

• 2 •

I see my former self, now a boy of eight years old, sitting on the high, back door step of Ivy Cottage. To the right is the corrugated, iron-roofed washhouse, with its brown stone sink, its wooden stopper and cold water tap, known as the 'Whiz Bang'. Beyond is the 'privee'. A ducket lavatory – distempered walls, sheets of damp, torn newspaper hanging from a rusty nail, and bench seat with a hole in the middle and a bucket beneath, emptied weekly by Mr Cliffe, the 'muck man', known locally, and affectionately, as 'Ashes of Cliffe'. And further still, the pigsty. Billy, the bad-tempered pig converted into bacon and replaced by a couple of tons of coal. On the railway side of the yard is a much corroded oil drum, placed strategically to collect rainwater from an even rustier down pipe secured merely by its connection to the rotting gutter above. Facing, is a black and white striped pigeon coot, empty now, built thirty or so years earlier by Uncle Harry. The paint is peeling and greying. A yellowing piece of lace curtain hangs limply in the small window – a reminder of the days, not long ago, when my cousin Doreen used it as a play house. It is one of those magical April days that seems to have been borrowed from late May. There I go, over the fence, into Weaver's field and onto the railway track. Running, skipping, tripping, stopping at the pond to search for sticklebacks and then to skim a piece of slate, picked up earlier for the purpose – one, two, three, four bounces before it disappears into the black depths – sending out an ever-widening circle of ripples before reaching the edge of the bank where I'm standing, and lapping briefly before settling, once again, into a murky stillness. I am startled by a thrush and I sink to the ground to study its antics. I see it settle for a moment on its untidy nest in the fork of a young birch. As it flies away, I creep up to the tree and stretch to reach the nest. I can feel four warm eggs. I take one and almost immediately I'm attacked by the incensed mother. I'm terrified and leg it back to the cottage hotly pursued by the irate bird. Later, I prick out holes at each end and blow the yellow life out of the egg onto the rough ground. I feel no pleasure. Indeed, I have a dreadful pang of conscience that stays with me for the rest of my life. It is my first act of cruelty and I am ashamed. I learn a hard lesson.

Now ten years old, I see myself once more stretching to reach each of the railway sleepers. I'm on my way up the steady incline to see Granddad, seventy two and still working at Leycett pit. I catch sight of a small hole beneath Leycett lane some fifty yards away on my right and cross the field to take a look. I discover that it's a small tunnel for a narrow gauge railway, now redundant, but built to haul trucks of clay from the quarry at Finney Green up to the brick works at the far side of the wharf. When empty, the trucks were released and, powered by gravity, sped down the track, through the tunnel and back to the quarry to be refilled. I cautiously pull back the brambles and step inside. It is pitch black. I hear a rustle and turn to make my escape; a multitude of flapping wings around my head. I'm driven by sheer terror to get outside. I have disturbed a colony of bats and I sit on the warm grass outside the tunnel entrance physically shaking and dusting the imaginary creatures from my being.

The scene evaporates and the cottage is once again reduced to a shed. The railway line has been filled in and the small bridge over it, long gone. The cottage garden is opposite, across the narrow lane. Vegetable gardening was Sam's main hobby. As a young man he toured the district with his pony and cart, selling fruit and vegetables before he eventually went to work in the pit. He loved his garden. There he is, taking a breather on the dilapidated old bench seat under the apple tree. He wipes his brow with a large white handkerchief and pushes his moustache up with the back of his hand. Auntie Beattie, Uncle George, their daughters Doreen and Anne have flitted to a house on The

Moss. The offer of a new house with modern facilities is too good an opportunity to miss. It is the first time in his long life that Sam has had to live on his own and he is visibly lonely. He smiles a little to disguise his emotion and looks at his cottage, his family home, and now just a place in which to spend his last few years. The white climbing rose is at its best, filling the space between the two sets of windows and half covering the 'S' that he says is for 'Sam', but is really the end of the tie bar holding the front and the back walls of the cottage together. He loves his family deeply and is so proud of them all. He thinks of his grandson, Harry, who never fails to come and see him at the pit. He recalls his last visit just a week ago. He'd been oiling the engines in the 'fan house'. Sam had done every unskilled job in the mining industry and working in the 'fan house' is an occupation reserved for miners too old to work underground. It is a stepping stone to retirement. Sam hears the door latch lift, looks up and sees his grandson. He's below average height, with brown hair cut short with a fringe, large blue eyes set in a round, open face and a mischievous smile that creates a wrinkle on the bridge of his nose. He is self-effacing, quiet, yet less so in familiar company. His reticence is more than counter-balanced by his acute inquisitiveness and apparent interest in almost everything, especially the adult world.

• 3 •

"Hello, Granddad!" he shouts cheerfully. "What's that you're doing?"

Sam tells him of the importance of carrying out routine maintenance on the giant machines. He explains that the large engines, driven by steam, force the life-supporting fresh air into every corner of the mine. There is a strong smell of machine oil. Sam's bottle of cold tea warming on the pitted casting, quivers almost imperceptibly, the only evidence of vibration in the building. Sam wipes his hands on a piece of oily rag and tells Harry that he has something to show him. He takes him to an old door, thick and chalky with distemper, and forces it open with his shoulder. When they are both through, he closes the door and they walk across a short cast iron bridge to another similar door. There is a tremendous, almost deafening rushing of air. Sam tells Harry that because of the immense down draught caused by the fan, it's physically impossible to open one door without the other being closed. They pass into a small store room and Sam stoops down and almost whispers to Harry that he is going to tell him a story that he mustn't repeat to anyone.

"Ah've brought thee in 'ere to tell thee somethin' that very few people know abite. Abite two 'ear' ago a man came into the 'fan house', 'e was cold and wet and 'ungry so ah gives him a cuppa tea and 'alf me snappin', 'e turned out to be a German prisoner-of-war who'd escaped from a concentration camp, 'e showed me a photo of 'is wife and kids and ah felt sorry for 'im and 'id 'im in this 'ere room for thrae wicks until 'e was strong enough to move on." Harry stared into his Granddad's eyes questioningly. It was barely twelve months since the end of the war. The Germans were the enemy. Harry's young life was littered with stories of the hardships created by cruel Germans. In his young mind all Germans should be shown no mercy. He asked his Granddad why he hadn't told the police.

"Well, ah'll tell thee lad," he replied. "Ah thought abite me fower lads in the fost war, and if they'd've been in trouble over theer, ah would'a liked somebody to'ave 'elped 'em."

Harry nodded imperceptibly with understanding. Sitting there in his garden Sam reflects on the recent conversation with his grandson. He is sad that three generations have been so affected by conflict and prays that Harry will not have to follow his own boys into some future war. His thoughts stray to another visit of Harry's and he smiles as he remembers it. Ivy cottage is attached to Weaver's farm. They breed beef and dairy cattle, fierce looking beasts with large horns and evil eyes. Farmer Weaver slaughters and butchers his own cattle and sells the meat in a small shop next to the milking shed. On the day in question, his son Les was driving the dairy herd down the narrow lane for milking just as Harry emerged from the front door of the cottage. For the first time Sam saw fear in the boy's eyes, before he turned on his heel and scrambled over the railway embankment to safety. He also recalls Harry just half an hour later, confidence restored, leaning on the stable door of the milk shed, watching Les milking the cows by hand and getting covered as Les squirted the warm creamy milk from the cow's teat full into the lad's face.

Sadly, the old cottage has returned to the pile of stones from which it was first built. The Tomkinson's who drew their first breath there, who were nurtured and who matured into adulthood within its walls, and then married from it, are no more. Only memories remain and those are fading fast.

Ivy Cottage was initially owned by the Lord Crewe estate. During the late fifties, it was bought by Uncle Harry so that Sam could live out his days there, free of rent and in relative security. In 1963, when Uncle Harry died, Mum and Dad bought it and kept it as a place to visit, to tend the garden and in which to reminisce. In 1984, when it became a burden to them, they sold it and, within a very short time, it was knocked down.

CHAPTER FIVE

RATIONING

• 1 •

'Don't touch that! It's poisonous.' I'd spent a lovely day with Mum at Ivy Cottage and we were standing at the bus stop, just a short distance from the Crewe Arms, waiting for the bus to take us to Newcastle and home. It was October 1943. We seemed to have been standing there forever. I'd been watching some ragged rooks float down like a bundle of tattered, black rags before settling on a group of mature oaks across the lane in Finney Green; a prelude to dark and sinister invaders from a foreign soil. They were calling to each other peevishly as if they too wished to be out of sight from the menaces of the night. The last of the day had hurriedly disappeared over the Cheshire Plain and the Welsh mountains with the devil at its back. There was a sharpness to the wind heralding ill tidings and announcing that winter was flexing its muscles. Its chill fingers pinched our noses, sought out the weaknesses in our Utility clothing before playing an ethereal air on the telephone lines across the road like some sort of Aeolian harp; the murmur of men's voices in the nearby pub and the ghostly scream of a London to Glasgow express shutting down as it coasted on the long incline to Crewe station, amplified by the clearness of the night, just added to the apprehension.

Already there was the distinctive and menacing intermittent throb of a German bomber. The searchlights at the Crewe locomotive works and the Rolls Royce aircraft factory probed the sky, briefly illuminating the fields of ghostly Barrage balloons hovering like a school of airborne whales. The staccato rattle of a lonely machine gun was drowned out by the mournful drone of a distant air raid siren.

Behind the bus stop I had been attracted to a cluster of bindweeds that had threaded their way through an arthritic, old hawthorn. The white, funnel-shaped flowers were sprinkled with summer dust and dampened with beads of evening dew, giving them a luminescent quality as if in defiance of the blackout. It was as I reached out to pluck one of the blooms that my mother shouted. I was taken aback. I'd never heard her raise her voice before, certainly not at me, and I was on the point of tears. She immediately consoled me, but that first reproach stayed with me for many years. It is only with the fullness of time that I have come to realise the anxiety she must have been feeling and the urgent need she had to be reunited with the rest of our family.

And, at last, the green, double-decker, Crosville bus chugged slowly round the corner, its hooded lights giving it a tired expression and its shadowy passengers like inanimate cardboard cut-outs seemed to be placed by the windows for effect.

• 2 •

The second-world war was declared when I was three years old on the third of September 1939, and continued until I was ten. Wartime was as normal a time to me as if I had been born at any other time. As children, we came to look upon the war as a natural state of things. We never missed anything because we'd never known anything different. However, there were two aspects of the war that have haunted me and have remained embedded in the heart of my innermost conscience.

The first was evacuees. New faces appeared quite regularly both at school and within the neighbourhood and then often disappeared without trace or reason. One of these was a boy of my age who was killed on 26 June 1940 when bombs fell on Gower Street in the first air raid to hit North Staffordshire . . . such an irony that he died of the cause from which his evacuation had meant to protect him. Another was Shirley Beams.

I was lying on the small patch of grass that had been designated as my play area in the back yard. I was stretched out on my stomach, knees bent and ankles crossed, examining my handful of hard-won shotties when an almost imperceptible movement disturbed me. As I looked up I saw a girl about my own age framed by the hole in the hedge. I had been so preoccupied that I was totally taken by surprise.

"Who're you?" I asked rather abruptly.

"Shirley," she answered shyly.

She had brown, curly hair with a big red ribbon, and traces of tears in her hazel eyes that were set in her round, open face with pink cheeks and dimples and lots of good-natured little dots about her chin. My word, she was a bonny little girl, and well-dressed too. She wore a short-sleeved white blouse that exposed her amply dimpled little elbows, and she had a red, tartan plaid skirt with braces. Tied to one of her buttonholes was a large, brown luggage label on which was written her name 'Shirley Beams'.

It was Spring 1943 and the war was raging on the home front. The Luftwaffe was causing devastation and mayhem in our major cities. The blitz was at its height. Shirley was one of thousands of children who had been evacuated to areas of comparative safety. Bemused, parcelled up, parted from their families, transported on congested trains, dumped at local schools, picked over by prospective guardians like cabbages in a greengrocer's basket, and carted off to live with strangers in an alien environment without so much as a by your leave – eight shillings and sixpence per week for each child. Children's views were not invited. They were not allowed to have opinions. Their feelings were not considered. They should be seen but not heard. Only adults were given these sorts of privileges. Children were less than people. It was enough that they would be safer away from the bombing, and that at least was true, but a little more humanity, understanding, counselling and consultation would have helped. After all children *are* people too.

"You been cryin'?" I asked.

"No," she fibbed, not wanting to admit to a weakness, or to share her loneliness with someone she didn't know.

"Where yer from?" I demanded without looking up or attempting to move from my comfortable position.

"London, I'm an evacuee," she responded, unsure as to whether it was something she should be proud of or not. "Want to see me shotties?" I volunteered.

"What are shotties?" she enquired uncertainly.

"These 'ere," I said.

"They look more like marbles to me," she replied with a sort of detached disinterest. She moved out of the hole in the hedge and came to sit beside me on the grass embracing her knees as she did so.

"This 'ere's me favourite. I call it Egg'n'bacon 'cause it's white with streaky red. These two are Cat's Eyes; they're me swaps, and this big stone one's Bull's Eye on account of its big black spot."

I showed her how to flirt them between the thumb and index finger, and how to play Killer. In between the high concentration required between shots we chattered like two little monkeys until I was called in for tea.

I told my mother about Shirley.

"Mum, she talks all la-di-dah, and calls a bath a 'barth' and says 'larst' for last and is Landon near London?"

My mother explained to me that people from different parts of the country spoke with different accents. She told me that Shirley would be living next door with Mrs. Higgins for the time being, and that Mrs. Higgins had asked if I could take Shirley to school with me in the morning.

I was considered to have a level of independence beyond my seven years. Like Dad, I was economical with the spoken word and could work things out for myself. My shirt sleeves were always rolled up and my socks down around my ankles exposing a multitude of scars and bruises from my various battles with gravity and Mother Nature.

Next morning I went round to Mrs Higgins and said "I've come to collect Shirley and Mum said make sure she's got her gas mask." We chatted all the way to the small school at the top of Croft Street. It was a very old school that had been condemned, but was saved by the war when the new school was requisitioned by the Royal Navy for the duration. I took Shirley to see my teacher, Miss Toft, as soon as we arrived.

"Please Miss, this is Shirley Beams and she's an evacuee."

"Thank you Harry. Please take her to the seat next to you. I want you to take care of her," she told me. I almost burst with pride at the big responsibility bestowed upon me by my very own favourite teacher. And I didn't shirk my duty. I shared the experience of my very short life with her. I showed her where to hang her coat and gas mask; where to stand so she wouldn't be picked out to fetch the milk; how to ease back the side of her gas mask with her finger so that she could breathe more easily on air raid practices; how to make paper pellets to shoot out of milk straws; who to, and who not to talk to. I became her sole guardian, her confidante and her constant companion.

Out of school she shared my secrets, lived my adventures and got to know my cherished hideouts.

I took her to Farmer Johnson's pig sty to show her the rat holes and on the way back we gathered a bunch of wild wood forget-me-nots from under the hedge. I borrowed one of my mother's bottling jars from the pantry to put the flowers in for her. We became firm friends. I used my coloured chalks to create a pattern on her top; made her a stick for my bowler; taught her to use my catapult and how to make arrows with a garden cane and a bent beer bottle top. She was Jane to my Tarzan; Minnie-Ha-Ha to my Hiawatha; Maid Marion to my Robin Hood. She helped me to shovel up the manure left behind by the Co-op milk-cart horse for Mrs. Hall's roses and we shared the two pence she gave me. I even succumbed to playing hopscotch and loaned her one of my special jacks made out of a piece of blue tile that I'd chipped out of the floor

A Staffordshire Lad

of the abandoned house at the top of the Ashfields New Road. More, I bore all the jibes from the kids in the next street when I tied one end of the skipping rope to the gate post and then held the other end while she skipped the day away.

One day I took her up to the railway and showed her how to make a penny out of a ha'penny by putting it on the line before the train came by. I taught her how to stand on the pig bin and swing on the gas lamp.

On wet days we'd sit under the kitchen table on the coconut mat and read comics. Shirley's favourites were Comic Cuts, Chicks Own, Film Fun, and the Dandy and Beano. She loved Stan and Ollie, Snitch and Snatch and Lord Snooty and his gang. Sometimes we'd sit in the kennel and count the dog's teeth.

Then one day she wasn't there. I'd popped round to call for her and all Mrs. Higgins had said was "Gone back!" and shut the door. I was devastated. I went home and said to my mother, "Mum, Shirley's not there, Mrs. Higgins says she's gone back and I haven't even said good bye."

"Her father came last night and took her back to her home. Now don't bother me and go out and play," my mother ordered with finality.

I picked up my bag of shotties from the old disused coal scuttle and went to my patch of grass. I'd not only lost my best friend, but also much of my sparkle. Somehow, my shotties didn't hold the magic they'd had and life wasn't so much fun any more. Eventually, my gaze fell on the gap in the hedge and I wished so much that Shirley was standing there as she had been that first time. And then something caught my eye and I went to have a look. It was Mum's bottling jar and in it was one of the forget-me-nots that I'd picked with Shirley. It had survived because it still had a root and was sitting in a drop of water at the bottom of the jar. I poked a hole in the soil and planted it. Over the years it spread and filled the gap in the hedge as a reminder of my young friend.

• 3 •

The second aspect of the war that greatly affected me was the 'bombing out' of families in nearby Wolstanton. Anderson shelters were allocated to alternate houses to be shared by two families. We were supposed to share with Key's, a neighbour of ours, but we didn't get on. I never found out why. With hindsight, I respect Mum and Dad's reluctance to tell me, and the fact that they never stopped me from talking to Kenneth and Glennis Key, but clearly, sharing the same shelter wasn't an option. So, when the air raid siren sounded, we were dragged out of bed and were huddled together in a corner of our ground floor bathroom, covered in blankets and filled up to the gunnels with piping hot cocoa. Bursting with a mixture of excitement and fear, we'd strain our ears to see who was first to hear the unmistakable sound of the German bombers. Mostly, the air raid warnings were false alarms, but one crisp, moonlit night Dad took me up to his bedroom and we saw three black shapes following the railway line. It was through this window that I had been hung unceremoniously on the day I was born and it was through the same window that I saw my first and only bombs dropped. Dad immediately scooped me up and raced downstairs to the others in the bathroom. Mum had her arms wrapped around the girls. We felt the floor tremble, but there were no explosions. We learned the following day that the bombs had failed to explode. There was a lot of military activity for the next couple of days until they were made safe.

Air raids were not all bad news. If the sirens hadn't sounded the all clear by eleven o'clock, school didn't start until ten the next morning. Bad news travelled fast. We heard within a few hours about the bombed out houses in Wolstanton and a few of us raced up to see them. Most of the tiles had been blown off the roofs; all the windows had been shattered; there were big craters in the gardens; mattresses were still smouldering where they'd been thrown out. I was mesmerised at the spectacle. An old lady came out of the nearest house. She was crying and asked politely for us to leave. I was profoundly moved. My initial excitement distilled into sadness for those poor people. So this was war. It wasn't all fun as I'd supposed. We left that sorry, devastated place and with it, the 'comfort zone' of being wrapped in cotton wool, the insulation and naiveté of youth. It could have been us.

"You won't get much in your stockin' this Christmas;" my first memory of the war. Although too young to appreciate its significance, it somehow stuck in my mind. It was the Sunday following the outbreak of war. I was three years old. Uncle Reg and Aunty Jessie came to visit us most weeks. They had three children, Jean, Wilf and Ken. They lived in a dark and dismal suite of rooms at the back of Blackburn's butchers in George Street, Newcastle. I suppose much of the conversation was about the war and Aunty Jessie had made this comment because of her concern as a mother, and because the coming Christmas was the first that I would attach some importance to.

The next couple of years were just a round of visiting and being visited by relations. My sisters, Joan and Mary, were both at school, so, during the day, it was just Mum and me, and, of course, Dad on Thursday afternoons. When it was anything like fine Dad was in his garden, but on very wet days, and only occasionally, I'd get taken to the pictures. If I was lucky it would be a western, or a Sabu film. Invariably it was something completely over my head and I just went to sleep. Going to the pictures was a way of life. There was a ceremony to it. It meant orderly queuing and measuring their length to estimate the time as to when, or whether we'd get in; staring into windows of uninteresting shops, making faces at my reflection; watching small boys who asked "can you take me in Mister?" when it was an 'A' film, feeling smug that I was with an adult, but storing it up so that I could try it out myself at a future date; arriving at the ticket office and peering through the glass as we were asked what we wanted, "nines at the front, shillings in the stalls and one and sixes in the circle," wondering at the empty sales counter as to what else it might have held other than a pile of sepia coloured 'Picturegoer' magazines; having our tickets punched by the attendant; shown to our seats by a beam from a torch; blinking to adjust to the darkness and stumbling up the miles of stairs; brushing past begrudging folk who had to stand, lift up their seats to let you through; subsiding thankfully into the seat; being told to fold up my Burberry and put it underneath, and to stop fidgeting; being complained at for wanting to go to the lavatory just as the film was starting; bombarded with all sorts of missiles from rich folks' kids in the circle; trying to get a better view between the heads of the two people in front determined to block out my view, and asking Dad if I could sit on my Mac' to raise me up a bit; bored with the Pearl and Dean adverts, especially the locals; perked up with the Pathe News and the war; dozed through Fred Astaire; on the edge of my seat through Hopalong Cassidy; blinking as my eyes adjusted to the brightness, and light-headed as I came out of a world of guns and bullets to the disappointingly mundane world of reality and sameness.

· 4 ·

It's Thursday afternoon now and I'm waiting for those familiar heavy footsteps in the yard that herald the arrival of my Granddad Sam. He's very special to me. He arrives, takes off his cap, ducks under the back kitchen doorway and fills the room with his physical presence and good humour. In one hand he clutches a white paper bag full of small ginger nuts the size of a penny, bought from Miss Toft's shop in Liverpool Road. He scoops me up with his free hand. Mum has the kettle simmering on the gas stove and before long has a cup of tea brewed for him. He lets me dunk my biscuit while holding my wrist to prevent my hand from being scalded and the biscuit from disintegrating into a soggy mass at the bottom of his cup.

He puts me down and I sit on my favourite seat, the iron shelf with my back to the oven door. He scolds me and says, "It'll dry up your marrer." I don't know what *marrer* is, but it seems to be an important part of my anatomy, so I move away instantly and make for the small pouf, which to a three year old is a large pouf and I am lifted on to it, and made comfortable so that I can listen to the conversation between Mum, Dad and Granddad. Before long my eyes focus on Granddad's feet. He's wearing long, woolly socks held up by multi-coloured garters knitted by various grandchildren, and big shiny black boots, the highlight of my fascination. His big black boots, probably size thirteen, occupy a large piece of lino'. I can't take my eyes off them. Surely, they are the mythical seven league boots; they are my sole interest; I'm closer to them than I am to his face; I long to have a pair just like them and beg Mum and Dad to buy me a pair. Somehow they manage it. I'm told 'they were the only ones of my size in the shop'. I am overjoyed.

I love the sound of my own feet. I clump everywhere in them. Mum has to go to the dentist's. She has pyorrhoea, a gum disease that causes puss to discharge from her gums, a common ailment. She has to have all her teeth taken out. The dentist is on the first floor of an old Victorian building in Merrial Street, Newcastle. Uncarpeted wooden stairs lead to a waiting room covered in lino', both surfaces ideally suited for testing out my new boots, and I make the most of it. It's the last thing Mum hears before going under.

• 5 •

Although the government had started preparations prior to the outbreak of the war, there is a scurry to get everything done. Everyone is issued with an identity card. We have ours on 22 May 1940. Each person has a unique national registration number. Mine is ORTA 228 – 5. Ration books are issued soon after. The front of the books include our names and addresses, our identity numbers, serial numbers and the regional food office from where they are issued, ours being Newcastle. Inside are the coupons. An adult's weekly ration in May 1941 is: three pints of milk, one shilling's worth of meat, two and a quarter ounces of tea, eight ounces of sugar, four ounces of bacon, six ounces of butter, two and quarter ounces of cooking fat, one and a quarter ounces of cheese and eight ounces of jam. We make our own damson jam. We save our sugar over the year and, in October, Dad gets lots of fruit from one of his customers. The annual ceremony of jam-making begins. The brass jam kettle is resurrected, dusted down and coated sparingly with a piece of butter to avoid sticking. The fruit is picked over to remove the stalks and washed by Mum and the girls. An equal ratio of fruit and sugar is put in the kettle and then the water added. Mum takes over. Somehow she seems to know just how long it takes; she spoons a bit onto a cold plate and, as it cools, pushes it with her finger to check the wrinkle. The jars are washed and warmed and, while filling, I'm busy licking the plate clean. Finally, the small circles of greaseproof paper, prepared earlier, are tied on to the tops of the jars with white twine and the jam is left to cool on the quarry tiles in the pantry before putting into storage under my bed.

The government control prices so that no shops can charge higher prices for food, or other goods. It's a means of getting fair shares for all. The Ministry of Food also encourages everyone to eat more healthily. Before the war, surveys had shown that the British population was undernourished, half of working class women were in poor health and eighty per cent of under-fives had some bone abnormality, ninety per cent having badly formed or decayed teeth. Consequently, school milk is provided as well as cod-liver oil and orange juice. It's poured into me each morning from a large spoon. I hate it. The cod-liver oil forms large globules as it floats on the orange juice like a mini oil slick. Later, the cod liver oil is emulsified into a mixture of malt extract and tastes like toffee. So much nicer. The government has also opened a number of British Restaurants where meals can be bought coupons free. The local one in Newcastle is adjacent to the library. The food is basic but good.

Everyone's encouraged to grow more food and eat more vegetables, "Dig for Victory" is the slogan. In schools there are posters of the cartoon characters Doctor Carrot and Potato Pete. From 1 June 1941 clothes, material and footwear are rationed. Everyone's issued with a clothing coupon book. Initially each person is issued with sixty-six coupons annually. Later it's reduced to forty-eight. Utility clothes

A Staffordshire Lad

and furniture are often designed by well-known experts to minimise wastage of materials. My first bed arrives and has the famous Utility brand stamped on the frame. Until this point I've had to sleep in my sisters' bed. I'm now promoted to having my own bed and bedroom

In November 1941, the government introduces a 'points rationing system', as well as ordinary rationing. Everyone's allowed sixteen points a month. The 'points ration book' is pink. A person can 'spend' their points on anything they like – the whole lot on one tin of salmon or, more thriftily, on a few tins of pilchards. Later on in the war we are introduced to tins of imported meat called Spam. It can be fried, battered or eaten cold on sandwiches. The National Wholemeal Loaf is not rationed. It's made up of eighty-six per cent extraction flour (that is, using nearly all the wheat including the husks). It's a dirty beige colour and it's not popular, but I like it.

> *So will I bow to dear brown bread?*
> *Because, as my wise rulers say,*
> *We shall save tonnage in this way,*
> *But let this point be understood –*
> *No man can tell me it is good.*
> *(A P Herbert)*

There's a black market, but we're not aware of it locally, although bartering is rife and swapping generally accepted – a quarter of tea for a piece of cheese, for example, and it's not unusual to borrow the odd cup of sugar, and the like, from neighbours.

Mum saves the dripping from Sunday's roast. When it's cooled, she scoops it off the top of the gravy and puts it into a white basin. It's used for cooking and frying chips as well as pasting on pieces of bread with a sprinkle of salt to keep the wolf from the door when we kids get home from school.

Everyone's issued with gas masks and have to carry them everywhere. They have a Perspex visor and a large filter at the front with tight fitting rubber straps at the back. Public air raid shelters have been built in Roberts Avenue and in locations throughout the town. The largest of these is in the basement of the Savoy cinema that later became the Billiards Hall.

• 6 •

Generally, Fridays are Mum's shopping days in Newcastle and occasionally she takes me into Droys biscuit shop for a treat. The biscuits are all kept in large cubic tins about a foot square with the lids open to tempt customers. There's one with assorted broken biscuits that are all Mum can afford. I *'firk'* for my favourite, Malted Milk. I nibble round the cow leaving it till last.

On rare occasions she takes me into Burgess' café by the Post Office in the Ironmarket for a cup of tea and a cake, and then we go to Hulse's in Merrial Street to pay her card for some piece of furniture she has on the club. Each evening as dusk approaches, the blackout curtains are drawn, otherwise the ARP Warden comes calling. Our local ARP Warden is Percy Wright from Orton Road. He's a local councillor and a bit of a 'misery guts'. I can't recall him ever having a smile on his face. His wife's a drudge who seems to have had the light of life extinguished from her. Occasionally, Percy arranges a neighbourhood fire drill; a bit of a fiasco. The hosepipe doesn't fit properly on to the standpipe and the pipe leaks like a sieve.

Our local siren's situated at the cotton factory that backs onto Orton Road. The warning's a fluctuating, oscillating sound whilst the all clear is continuous.

A Staffordshire Lad

One late summer afternoon in 1943 the local and military police arrive on the front apparently looking for an AWOL (absent without leave) soldier. It's rumoured that he's hiding out in the wheat fields. We hare up to Mum's bedroom to have a look through, that same window. We can't see anyone, just the wheat where it's been trampled down. After a while he's spotted making a run for it; then he's caught and brought to the armoured car by our house. Old Mrs. Allman, our next-door neighbour, whose sons are in the war, shouts at the police asking for them to leave the poor man alone. But they ignore her and take him away.

The following week Percy Johnson's haystack catches fire. Eventually the fire engine arrives. The field is swarming with frustrated firemen and admiring kids. I'm one of them. The firemen, resplendent in blue uniforms and yellow helmets, fight the intense heat and flames, and eventually get it under control. I'm impressed and want to be a fireman.

In 1944 the Americans arrive in Newcastle and are based at Keele Hall. We see them coming down Roberts Avenue in their personnel carriers and we cheer and run beside the vehicles. The soldiers throw out handfuls of sweets, chewing gum and biscuits. Things we've only heard about and seen on the pictures. The biscuits are a kind of oatmeal block and I love them.

Now and again troops of soldiers are marched through the streets and we tramp along with them on the pavements trying to keep in step. I want to be a soldier.

One day, Mum and I are waiting for the Madeley bus at the Crosville bus stop outside Woolworth's in Newcastle. A Royal Air Force articulated lorry, of the type used for carrying large aeroplane sections, speeds round the bend into the High Street. A massive wheel it is transporting comes off and heads straight for me. I'm rooted to the spot, but Mum has the presence of mind to pull me out of the way. It completely demolishes the front of the shop, but fortunately we are unharmed.

The end of the war in 1945 brings many activities to celebrate VE Day (Victory in Europe Day). Flags and buntings are hung out of windows; some areas have street parties; dances and sports days are organised. Our local sports day is held in the field at the bottom of Roberts Avenue. There's a maypole and a band and races. My eldest sister, Joan, picks up half-a-crown for winning the girls' sprint. At a talent show in the Municipal Hall, Glennis Key sings 'Alice Blue Gown' and comes third. Arnold Roberts takes Graham and I to RAF Tern Hill, near Market Drayton to see the Air Show. We see the new twin-boomed Vampires and a Lancaster bomber flying on one engine. I want to be a pilot.

CHAPTER SIX

MINING

• 1 •

My young life revolves around 'Aidley, Madeley, Kale and Castle'. I hate 57 Diglake Street, Audley, the birthplace of my father and my sister Joan, and the home of Grandma and Granddad Titley. Throughout my growing up years, it's the place I least want to be. Mum, born in Madeley, shares my dislike, but for reasons associated with her unhappiness when she lived there after her marriage. Mary was born at Keele when Mum and Dad moved into their first home at Number One, Quarry Bank, a new, flat-roofed, concrete house. They only lived there for three years before flitting to Newcastle just before I was born.

I waste too many precious Saturdays in Audley. Joan takes Mary and me to the bus stop outside the chapel at the top of King Street. We catch the Mainwaring's bus to Audley, which takes about twenty-five minutes. Mainwaring Brothers are an independently owned bus service operating between Audley and Newcastle. The bus depot is situated at the bottom of Delph Lane in Bignall-End. The buses have both a driver and a conductor. The conductor calls out the name of each stop – Milehouse; the Hollows; Victoria Street; the Dragon; Springwood; White Rails; the Station; Ravens Lane; the Pump. I steadily become more and more depressed the nearer I get to it the Pump, our stop, so called because, before mains water supplies, it had been the central watering point for the area.

The house is semi-detached with an entry, unusual for a terrace type. There's no hot water or electricity; just gas-lighting and a coal fire for heating. The rooms are Victorian with expensive drapes and furniture including a high sofa. No-one, but no-one is allowed to sit on it. The house has a deep, dark cellar used for storage and refuge from bombs and thunderstorms!

Dad's the only child of Mary and Arthur Titley. He was born on 8 September 1905. His mother, Mary Carter, affectionately known to some as Molly and to others as Polly, conceived Dad out of wedlock when she was only fifteen. Granddad Arthur was seven years older and the event caused not a little upset in the Carter family. However, they married and live a relatively contented life. Molly is a person who appreciates the good things in life in spite of her poor health. Chapel, the August wakes and a Sunday evening stroll around the lanes are her only outings.

Arthur is quite a small man, about five feet four inches, but has exceptional upper body strength. He used to be a miner as were his father, Tom, and his brothers. Life in the mining community where he lived was hard and fraught with danger. Sons followed fathers into the mines and sometimes as many as three generations worked together, shoulder to shoulder, until they became too weak or too old to work, often dying at the pit face.

• 2 •

During the nineteenth and early twentieth centuries the coalmines were in private ownership. The Diglake Pits, where Granddad worked, were owned by W Rigby and Company. They worked on 'the Butty system' where miners were employed by a contractor and not by the owner. It worked similarly to current day farming practices, where the contractor is responsible for hiring and firing and for the provision of the tools and animals. Competition for Buttyships was keen and the margin of profit narrow, resulting in an element of risk and danger.

Mining was the main industry and the local pits had a catchment area that included Wood Lane, Miles Green, Bignall-End, Audley, Wereton, Alsagers Bank and Halmerend; a cluster of villages situated to the west of Talke 'O The Hill overlooking the Cheshire Plain; a group of small communities whose existence totally depended upon the local pit that had spread its black tentacles beneath their homes, their gardens and the surrounding countryside.

Arthur was born to be a miner. His physique was moulded to his occupation; short, bent, muscular. He joined the pit as soon as he left school. He'd never considered any other job. It would have been sheer heresy to have even thought of it in this community. He joined a band of hard working, dedicated, devout and fearless men, proud of their independence and content in the knowledge that the few bob they earned each day would provide a living to sustain both themselves and their families.

Typically, his working day started in the early hours with Molly up first to riddle out the ashes into the 'S' hole, start the fire and cut up his 'snappin'. If he was lucky, the thick crusty bread would be covered with the remnants of the previous day's rabbit stew, but more often than not it was plastered in a thick layer of salty dripping left over from Sunday's mutton. As he left home, he'd see shadowy figures behind the curtains of the smoke-blackened terraced houses, silhouetted by the dim, flickering light of candles and oil lamps. He'd be joined by his neighbours and their sons as they emerged from their homes; the tips and studs of their clogs and pit timps striking a rhythmic clatter on the rough cobbled streets. They wore flat caps; make and mend jackets with 'rabbit' pockets sown inside for the 'snappin' and bottles of cold tea, or water; singlets; coarse shirts and trousers; waistcoats and scarves. The young boys, miniature replicas of their fathers, would chatter in unbroken voices like a flock of sparrows. The closer to the pit, the more the number swelled, and then the mass of humanity, like a colony of ants, would be sucked, like a vortex, into the bowels of the cavernous and rapacious black earth.

The Fireman would hand out a Davy lamp, with its unique number, to each miner before he stepped into the cage. The Winder eased up the safety latch and the cage would plummet down to the pit bottom; the new boys catching their stomachs in their throats. When the cage disgorged its load on to the plate, the Hooker would signal the Banksman to let him know he was clear for the next batch. The men and boys, their eyesight gradually adjusting to the dark, would then make their several ways to the workplace, sometimes two or three miles distant. Conditions were unpleasant and dirty. The nearer to the coalface, the hotter and more humid it became. Arthur would strip to the waist and hang his 'snappin'-filled jacket high on a pit prop nail, secure from the hungry ponies and even hungrier mice. With his lamp hooked on to his leather belt, he'd work in cramped conditions, cutting the coal with his pick, the sweat making rivulets through the thick, black dust on his body before finding its way into his boots. Small boys worked with the pony drivers; coupling the tubs; placing the 'drags' to stop the 'journeys' from running back; opening and closing the doors, and generally helping with the ponies. There was the welcome break when the gangs settled down to eat; the print from the newspaper and the dust from their hands discolouring their food; the desire to drink more than their ration, and the discipline, born through experience, to save some till later.

The shift at an end, Arthur and the other weary miners would wend their way back to the cage and then to their several homes, often in darkness; the whiteness of their eyes belying their invisibility and the coughing up and spitting out of the coal dust-encrusted phlegm, together with the clatter of their feet, announcing their existence. A few hours earlier, as if by common consent, the kitchen chimneys belched out their smoke, signalling the men folk's return, whilst the fires busily heated the water in the coppers. The tin baths were placed in front of the hobs, filled with hot water a little kept back so that the men's clothes could be washed out in the dolly tubs with bar soap before hanging them on the clothes maids for drying and repair, whilst the men slipped out to wash the dust from their throats at the local pub prior to their evening meal.

As a fourteen year old, Arthur became quite a local hero by saving many of his workmates in the Diglake Disaster when the mine flooded. This is taken from a local report at the time.

'About two hundred and sixty men and boys were at work at the Diglake Pits' three coal seams, the Seven Feet, Eight Feet and Ten Feet. Workings. The Seven Feet and Ten Feet were to the east, or rise side of the shafts, whilst those in the

Eight Feet were to the west or dip side. The coal seams' dip to the southwest was at a gradient of one in three.

At about 11.40 a.m., the men working in the Ten Feet seam suddenly tapped an enormous body of underground water, believed to have been contained in old workings above the levels now being worked, but abandoned many years previously. The water, when released, rushed down the Ten Feet dips towards the shafts, in a torrent described as three feet high and of great velocity, carrying timber and pit wagons before it. At least one boy was carried down the length of the dip by the flood, and was amazingly rescued by a man at the bottom and pulled to safety. The water quickly reached the pit bottom roadways of numbers one and two shafts filling them to almost roof level before overflowing into the lower workings in the Eight Feet seam. Thus, the men working in the higher workings in the Ten Feet and Seven Feet seams were immediately cut off from the shafts and, in spite of heroic attempts at rescue, none survived except the one boy who was carried down by the flood.

Workers in the pit bottom area and in the lower Eight Feet workings had very little warning of the danger. They were not cut off from escape as the water rushed past them because the number three shaft, situated at Boyles Hall, was at a much higher level and was accessible to those who knew the way by an incline drift. Many men escaped by wading and even swimming to reach the drift. It was the first of these men who brought the news of the disaster to the surface.

The colliery under-manager, William Dodd, was in the pit in the vicinity of the Diglake Shafts when the water came in and as it was clearly impossible to reach the higher workings against the flow, he concentrated on organising the rescue of the men from the Eight Feet seam. Together with John Boulton, he moved around the area directing and helping

A Staffordshire Lad

the men to safety. Some had to wade through deep water and climb the ladders up a short shaft with water pouring down on them. The two men worked in conditions of great danger and almost complete darkness. As a result of their efforts twenty-seven men survived.

William Dodd received the Albert Medal from Queen Victoria at Windsor Castle on 9 March for his bravery. Others recommended for the Royal Humane Society award included John Boulton, John Johnson, John Watts (the colliery manager), Joseph Batemen and Amos Hinckley. William Dodd died twelve years later on 9 January 1907 having suffered recurring illness as a consequence of his experience. It is believed that he became unconscious several times as a result of his exertions in the icy water before he finally ascended the Boyles Hall shaft.

By five p.m. all the men who could be reached had been brought to the surface. Some confusion existed as to exactly how many men remained, but a final count revealed that seventy-five men and boys were missing. It was thought that many of these would be safe from immediate danger of drowning though cut off from escape.

The emotions of the waiting relatives can only be imagined; some families had several members underground and, during the first night, hundreds waited in the bitter winter weather at the pithead for news of their relatives. The crowds moved backwards and forwards over the snow between the Diglake and Boyles Hall shafts as rumours of rescue spread. The dismal appearance of the scene was heightened by the fact that the Inspectors of Mines forbade all naked lights at the pitheads in order to minimise the possibility of explosion from inflammable gas escaping from the shafts when the ventilation was restricted. The faint flickering miners' lamps were the only illumination for the waiting crowds.

One young woman refused to believe that there was no hope of any further rescues and kept a silent, anxious and lonely vigil from the engine house. She knew that her man worked in one of the lower levels. The engine-man and other workmen knew this and tried to persuade her to go home. She absolutely refused to go or to have any refreshment. Mrs. Sproston of Wood Lane, whose husband and two sons were still entombed in the mine, was in a dreadful state of hysteria. She seemed unable to understand any question addressed to her. The distressed woman reclined in a rocking chair unable to move and occasionally saying that she wanted to go to her husband and lads in the pit.

Pumping took place at all the shafts in an effort to lower the water level so that the trapped men could be reached. A large pump in the pit bottom could not be used as it was totally immersed and the shaft pumps made little or no impression. Men worked in relays to clear a way through the debris often up to their chests in water. From the Boyles Hall drift efforts were made to channel the water into the disused Eight Feet workings. These operations took several days.

By Saturday morning, 19 January, the water level had subsided somewhat, and a way was forced through the debris to the bottom of the Ten Feet main rise dip, which was found to be completely blocked by rubble. This however, was holding back a great volume of water from the higher workings. A further risk was from noxious gasses forced from the old workings by the water and affecting the area so much that further rescue work was too dangerous and rescuers were withdrawn'.

Arthur's father Tom, my great-grandfather, waited three days and three nights at the pithead for news of his son Tom and was convinced that he could still hear tapping on the pipes when the decision was made to seal the pit off.

A Staffordshire Lad

Tom was one of the seventy five registered as lost. Only two bodies were recovered and these during the first two days. Thirty-eight years later, in August 1933, miners from the adjacent Rookery Pit, broke through into the Diglake Ten Feet workings and recovered three more bodies. It was apparent that they had not died from drowning, but from suffocation when the flood cut off the ventilation. The remaining seventy bodies were allowed to remain entombed in the pit where they had died. A national fund for the dependants of the victims was launched, which realised £14,926.

• 3 •

Grandma's feelings towards the three of us vary to the extreme. Joan is useful and Grandma wants to adopt her. She uses her unmercifully to do both her own chores and errands, and those of her friends and relations. She worships Mary and in her feels herself personified. She has no time for me at all. She sends me anywhere to get rid of me; more often to Mrs. Harrison's across the brick bank to get a couple of mantles for the gas lights with strict instructions to carry them carefully to avoid breaking them. Mrs. Harrison has converted her parlour into a 'shop' to sell essential goods to the 'street'.

At lunchtime we are sent to Betty's, the local chip shop, for a basin of chips and mushy peas to be shared between the four of us. In the afternoon we go to The Palace, formerly the Coronation Picture Palace opened in 1911, and affectionately known to everyone as the 'Tu'penny Rush'. We avoid the wooden seats at the front and keep our heads down when the feisty Mrs Plant, with wavering torch, winkles out the trouble-makers. On the way home we stroll through the woodland walk at Town Fields to Old Road. We stir the water in the hollow of an old oak tree and make our wishes.

Like many miners, Granddad supplements his income by keeping hens. He keeps upwards of two hundred fowl, trekking twice daily from home up to his Delph Lane smallholding to feed and care for them. He sells the eggs locally and the cockerels for Christmas. His favourite breeds are Rhode Island Reds, Black Leg Horn and White Sussex, and occasionally he keeps a few geese and bantams. His family, hens, a pipe full of strong Twist and the Sunday evening service on the wireless are his only interests. He's strong 'chapel', and has been a warden for many years. When I'm older, he asks me for some help with his fowl. The laying hens are kept in triangular-shaped coots and, at their best, lay an egg every day. I help collect the eggs in an old straw-lined bucket. I love the touch of a newly laid egg and the feel of a day old chick. Eggs are hatched in an incubator and occasionally Granddad brings some into the house to be kept warm by the fire. The fowl are fed twice each day. In the morning they have a mix of meal and old vegetables and potato *'pillings'* that have been boiled up on the hob. In the afternoon they have wheat grain. The rest of the time they just scratch about in the grass. At night they have to be fastened up in the coots to protect them from the foxes.

Granddad is a very experienced poultry farmer and recognises the symptoms immediately when anything is wrong. Fowl that go off their laying are either broody, or have picked up *'feg'*, an indigestible rye grass that decomposes in the crop. I hold the hen by its legs on its back while Granddad slits the crop with a razor blade. He pulls the *'feg'* out with his fingers then sews up the crop with strong wax cotton. Surprisingly, it has little affect on the fowl and they just go clucking off to their mates, returning to full production within a few days.

Piercing between the ears with an old pair of scissors to kill the older hens that are passed their sell by date is general practice. Their legs are then tied together and hung on a nail in the back yard, the blood draining into an old zinc baby bath. After dressing, they are part boiled and roasted to tenderise the meat. A few cockerels and geese are also reared for the table.

CHAPTER SEVEN

LEARNING - RYE CROFT SCHOOL

• 1 •

Early in September 1941, Graham and I start to school. Both our mums take us on the first day, thereafter alternating. Situated at the top of Croft Street, Rye Croft school is about a twenty minute walk from home. Condemned before the war and reprieved to save costs, the school has very poor facilities. Most of the space in the schoolyard has been used to build air raid shelters leaving little room for recreation and physical education. The shelters are camouflaged on the outside and whitewashed inside with small lanterns to provide the minimum of light. The classrooms are dark with high windows designed to deter daydreaming, covered with anti-shatter paint to protect from flying glass in the event of an air raid, and fitted with very dark curtains for the blackout. In spite of all these measures, the lights are never switched on. When the light becomes too bad, lessons are re-organised. Desks are fixed benches with holes for the inkwells, no drawers and long benches to sit on. The teachers are Miss Toft, Miss Cook and Miss Hunt. My favourite, Miss Toft, also owns a confectionary shop in Liverpool Road where Granddad buys his ginger nuts. She is mild-mannered, softly spoken, and protective. She is someone in whom I can confide; she is to be my school-time mother, that is in my imagination, to give me comfort. All three teachers wear, three-quarter length floral smocks over their day clothes. The senior teacher is Miss Goodwin who dies suddenly in December 1943. The position is filled by Miss Hassalls where she stays until her retirement in 1948.

We have packed sandwiches for lunch and occasionally, as a treat, some cocoa powder mixed with sugar. No dining room. We sit on the hot cast iron pipes in the hall when it's cold and in the playground when it isn't.

My time at Rye Croft seems to be a succession of gas mask drills; walking single file into the air raid shelters; packed in like sardines – death by gas or suffocation! Usually assemblies are followed by singing traditional songs to swell our chests such as 'Oh God our help in ages past', and 'All people that on earth do dwell'. We are encouraged to have pride in our country. Our teachers and parents engender a mood of nationalism. 'British to the backbone' we shout as we slap our right elbows into our left hands.

Evacuees come from Lancashire and the Midlands as well as from London, as did Shirley Beams; the latter mainly to escape the flying bomb attacks in 1944. Hassell Street school hall is converted into a dormitory for late arrivals prior to their relocation to families. The school also has an evacuee teacher to help with billeting.

· 2 ·

We are ever conscious of the war effort. It is a constant national preoccupation that pervades most aspects of our lives. The sale of war savings stamps is an important school activity. There are national fund-raising weeks starting with 'War Weapons Week' and 'Warship Week in 1941'. 'Wings for Victory Week' in 1943 and 'Salute the Soldier Week' in 1944, also important events. As well as money-raising activities, we have to collect jam jars and newspapers to take to school for salvage. The girls knit for the navy. We also collect books and magazines for the armed forces. Dependant upon how many books we collect determines what rank we become. We can be 'promoted' from Lance Corporal through the ranks to senior officer status.

Air raids play havoc with attendance due to the interruption and loss of sleep. Fortunately, both Rye Croft and my next school, Hassell Street, are untouched by bombs. Early in the war, the Westlands Girls senior school has to move into Hassell Street because the Fleet Air Arm has requisitioned the school. This means that Rye Croft has to be used for infants and juniors until the war is over. In January 1946 we move to Hassell Street to form a new mixed junior school.

CHAPTER EIGHT

LEARNING - HASSELL STREET SCHOOL

• 1 •

'Hushaby Scary,
Don't be contrary!
Turnips will nip you unless you are good!
Worzels will worzel
And furzles will furzel;
Bogles will fetch you, unless you are good.'

The bogeyman terrorises my waking hours; it is my imaginary horror. It hides inside the house; under the bed; in the coalhouse; at the back of the coats in the hall; in the pantry; under the table; behind the curtain that hangs under the sink and moves suspiciously when least expected; it makes the stairs creak. Doors have to be pushed fully open before I have the courage to go through. Definitely black with large, lifeless eyes. It can move, but not as fast as me. I never fail to beat it to the back door. It never goes outside. Outside I am quite safe.

'Worzel Gummige' by Barbara Euphan Todd. "I'm Worzel Gummige. I chose the name this morning. My granfer's name was Bogle." I am unaware that *bogle* is an archaic word for bogeyman, but it is near enough to scare me out of my wits when Mrs. Slaney reads out this poem to the class one Friday afternoon. She is to be my last teacher in primary, and although only at Hassell Street for eighteen months, they are to be some of the happiest of my school days.

The move to Hassell Street takes place in January 1946. There have been considerable staff changes due to the war, but with the coming of peace, the school is reorganised to form a new mixed junior school under the headship of Mr Showan. There are four hundred and eighty pupils including one hundred and twenty who are still at Rye Croft. Mr White, teaches music. He has recently returned from the war. A new teacher, Mr Burgess, a great cricketer who plays for Audley and Staffordshire, joins the staff. For the first six months I am in Form 3A. and my teacher is Mr Holland. He is a small, jolly, portly, bald-headed, middle-aged man who talks and chuckles through his teeth. In September 1946 I move up to the top class, 4A, where Mrs Slaney is the teacher. And it is in the early part of 1946 that we gratefully hand in our gas masks ; the air raid shelters are sealed off and used only for storage.

Mrs. Slaney is a gem, assuredly the most influential teacher I shall ever have. The sister-in-law of a former staff member, Mr Dick Slaney, she has been teaching at the school since 1940 and will continue until 1960. She is middle-aged, wears glasses, has crinkly hair and wears the obligatory floral smock overall. She rules from behind her tall desk from which she rarely emerges. Mrs Slaney is firm, fair and, at times, funny. Her quietly forceful manner commands respect. She has the ability to identify her pupils' assets and build on them. She opens my eyes to the treasures of literature and sparks my imagination for stories of adventure. She is able to get the best out of us with words rather than threats. She awakens my intellect and I am launched into a world of literary heroes.

However, she threatens that she won't read another chapter of *'Worzel Gummige'* on Friday afternoons *'unless we are good'*. Forty kids sit for half an hour every Friday afternoon totally absorbed in the story of a magic scarecrow that comes to life; young minds hang on to every word; minds as yet without the clutter of adult life, soaking it all up like blotting paper. I live each moment; I am there in Ten-acre field at Scatterbrook. I find myself subconsciously, gently patting my jacket pocket expecting to feel a robin and its family deep inside. I admit to being one of those who sheds tears when John and Susan wave goodbye to Worzel from the train at the end of the book. It is this story that, whets my interest in natural history.

• 2 •

For the first time since starting to school, I am separated from Graham who is put into the B stream. I miss him a lot, but we remain the best of friends. I quickly become friendly with my new classmates. Jimmy Hanley, from Albany Road, Harry Minshull, whose parents own the chip shop opposite The Hanging Gate public house at the top of Hassam Avenue; Graham Amphlett; Brian Tinsley; Geoffrey Allman; Ray Evans; Eric Fletcher; Ivan Bates; John Bowler; Jimmy Ryles; John Garthwaite; Peter Mellanchip; Elvie Lindop whose parents own the butchers in Liverpool Road outside

A Staffordshire Lad

of which Joan gets knocked down by a car on her way home from school and is taken into Lindop's quite shaken, but is more concerned about her torn coat than her injuries. Elvie's family emigrate to Canada in August 1947. There are also Jean Simpkin; Evelyn Peake; Hilda Lawton whose parents own the corner shop in Charter Road; and Jean Palmer, the smallest in the class.

Jimmy Hanley introduces me to 'the tuppenny rush', the Saturday morning picture show for kids. I call for Jimmy at his home in Albany Road about half past eight. First stop is at Walter Tryner's paper shop at the top of Roberts Avenue to buy the Daily Mirror, fly to the back page and tear out the photographs of our favourite footballers to be stuck into our scrapbooks later. We then walk into Newcastle and catch the Hanley bus outside Marsden's tailors in the Ironmarket, a journey of about twenty minutes, arriving at the Odeon cinema about half past nine. The cinema overflows with kids from all over the Potteries. We sing songs like:

> *We come along on Saturday morning*
> *Greeting everybody with a smile*
> *We come along on Saturday morning*
> *Knowing it's well worthwhile*
> *As members of the Odeon club we all intend to be*
> *Good citizens when we grow up*
> *And champions of the free*
> *We come along on Saturday morning*
> *Greeting everybody with a smile, smile, smile*
> *Greeting everybody with a smile*

Talent contests are part of the fun and, on birthdays, club birthday cards and free passes are given out. The inevitable Flash Gordon or a Buck Rogers serial with boos for the villains

A Staffordshire Lad

and cheers for heroes followed with films including Laurel and Hardy, Old Mother Riley and The Three Stooges.

After the show we scurry home for dinner, meet up again at Jimmy's about 1.30 and walk into Stoke for the football match at the Victoria ground. We worship our idols, Stanley Matthews, Freddy 'Nobby' Steele and Neil Franklin, all England players.

Mrs. Slaney cherishes all kinds of flowers, especially wild ones. We all know it; each one of the Standard Four A pupils know it. One or the other of us is forever bringing her a bunch when the seasons allow. There's never a time when the glass vase that sits on the side of her desk is empty. Even in December and January it's filled with a selection of dried cow parsley, teasel and beech. She never lets on that she would prefer us to leave them to grow happily in their natural habitat; she wouldn't hurt our feelings for the entire world, but one day she is noticeably upset.

It's just after assembly on a warm May morning and Elvie Lindop presents her with a large bunch of bluebells. After thanking Elvie she asks her to return to her seat. It's clear to us all that Mrs. Slaney is troubled and she says emotionally, "I want you all to listen to what I am going to tell you."

"Many years ago, when I was not much older than you, I used to spend my summer holidays with my grandmother who lived in the country. Most of my time was occupied in exploring the countryside and picnicking on the heath with my brothers and the three children from the cottage next door.

Each morning we'd pack a picnic in an old army surplus haversack. Our friends from next door insisted that we each take our note books and coloured pencils to make copies of the wild flowers that we saw on our expeditions. We became expert at recognising all the different types. Then one very hot dry summer, the heath caught fire. It was completely burned out, the grey, ominous smoke hung over the countryside for days and all life was wiped out.

No-one knew how the fire had started, but suspicion pointed to a group of young teenagers who'd been known to use the heath to smoke cigarettes. Perhaps it was a lighted match, or a cigarette end, that had caused so much devastation. Such a simple mindless act may have resulted in the tragedy. We were never able to enjoy that dear place again. By the time it recovered we were all grown up and pursuing our separate lives.

Of course, there were other places to explore and one of our favourites was the bluebell wood. The wood was centuries old and filled with oak and elm and beech. It was part of the Manor estate and we had to climb an old sandstone block wall to get into it. It was a magical place. The ground was covered in a thick rich depth of leaf mould which in May time was carpeted completely in masses of bluebells. The perfume was overwhelming. There were also clumps of wood anemone and drifts of wild garlic.

Each May Day children from the local villages used to descend on the wood. Like us, they would take picnics and spend the day there. They'd gather armfuls of bluebells to take home, or to take to school, just like Elvie has done. And just like Elvie, instead of snapping the stalks at ground level, most of them pulled the flower from the bulb." She holds the bluebells up to show us the white stalks. She tells us that when this happens, the bulb dies, and that most of the bluebells in the wood had died this way.

• 3 •

New aspects are introduced to the curriculum. Swimming instruction at Newcastle baths, just a couple of hundred yards away from the school; music lessons with Norman White who forms a percussion orchestra with the class. He plays the piano and the rest of us bash tambourines and triangles; the sheer dread I feel knowing I am about to hit my large triangle at the wrong time and seeing Mr White holding his head in his hands through total frustration at my lack of coordination; the relief when he gives it to someone else and music lessons suddenly became more acceptable. As well as music Mr White is known for his precise handwriting, like copperplate, especially on the board.

Mr Showan, the Headmaster, is a mild-mannered man. He will have been head teacher for thirty-one years when he retires in 1963 and has served as a teacher at the school for many years beforehand. He has an olive green, coach built Wolesley car, which he parks on the narrow strip between Barracks Road and the front of the school. Graham and I drool over it, fascinated by the badge on the bonnet that lights up when the ignition is switched on.

Mrs Slaney encourages us all to join the library and as a result I am introduced to Squadron Leader Bigglesworth, 'Biggles', the airborne Homeric hero, fashioned by the author Captain W.E. Johns. I decide that I am definitely going to be a pilot. I read all his books including the 'Gimlet' series, Biggles' army commando equivalent, and also the 'Worrals' series, the female version, but with less passion. I search for any book with a cover showing an aeroplane. I exhaust the supply of them in Newcastle library. I turn to The Hardy Boys' books. They are the sons of an American detective who inevitably become involved in solving crimes themselves. I also read 'The Lost World' and for the rest of my life become fascinated with South America, and in particular, the Amazon forest. Dad buys me Fennimore Cooper's 'The Last of the Mohicans' and I

A Staffordshire Lad

spend many happy hours being chased through the Canadian forests by bands of wild Huron savages.

During this final year at Hassell Street, I discover I have an ability to run at speed. The physical training exercises in the playground are always followed by speed games. In spite of being small and scrawny, it satisfies me that I can outstrip everyone in the school. I develop a strong competitive attitude. Although not a talented player, I'm selected to play for the school football team, a great honour. We compete against other local junior schools. The matches are played on the Orme Road playing fields on Saturday mornings. Mrs. Slaney, always interested in the results, offers half-a-crown to the goal scorers, a substantial amount in those days. I play right full back, a position that is only played in the defender's own half. The only way I can score a goal is through my own net, a point I put to Mrs Slaney. She doesn't bite.

I am also given a part in the school play, 'Dotheboys' Hall', taken from Charles Dickens' 'Nicholas Nickleby'. I play 'the small boy' who sits at the end of the row, says nothing and gets clouted unceremoniously, and regularly, for the sheer hell of it. Evelyn Peake, the tallest and heftiest girl in the school is Mrs Squeers and metes out the punishment with sadistic delight.

The winter of 1947 is one of the worst on record with heavy snow and severe cold. At times, throughout January and February, attendance is down to fifty per cent and, much to our delight, the school closes for one week due to the fuel crisis. There is no coke for the boiler and the electricity is cut off for most of the day.

On our way home, more often than not, we are drawn by the strong, sweet smell of boiled sweets that are made at the local Betty Plant's factory near Croft Street. The main manufacturing base is in Hanley. We cluster round the open door, jockeying for a good position and look down, mouths watering, on the large, steaming copper vats attended by women draped in sack bags and wearing turbans. They use large wooden spoons to stir the sugar and glucose. The mixture is rolled flat and squeezed through a tube before being cut up and wrapped. All sorts of sweets are made including herbal cough sweets, sugared almonds, spearmint chews and dairy mints. The Stoke based business was originally named after the owner's mother, Elizabeth Plant.

Occasionally I walk home alone and take a different route. Inevitably, I am attracted to the level crossing at the Brampton and, in particular to the signal box there. The signalman, Mr. Bond, seems as though he is always waiting for me and has the battered, steel kettle singing its plaintive song on the black cast iron stove.

Mr. Bond is our next door neighbour but three. His home is at the other end of our block of four. He is married, but has no children. He is a tall, straight man with deep-set, bright, unwinking blue eyes that radiate intelligence. He is a well-respected man and a Newcastle borough councillor having recently completed his term as Lord Mayor of the town. He wears the traditional L.M.S. black serge uniform that has seen too much service and too little cleaning, and is in sad contrast to the gleaming brass buttons that run down the front of his tunic. His cap is as shiny with handling as the seat of his pants are with sitting, though neither can compete with the large shiny hunter watch that he keeps in his waistcoat pocket. It's attached to a thick silver chain bedecked with an array of small medals awarded to him as a young man for a variety of sporting achievements. As each train passes the signal outside the box, he holds the watch with its hinged silver lid fully open in his outstretched hand as if demanding the train to argue with him that the watch is wrong and not *it* that's a minute or so late, or early, before he turns to 'book in' the details in the register. He beckons to me. I race up the eleven steps two at a time. Passing through the signal box door I am greeted with a combination of unique and half-forgotten smells. Most prevalent is the Ronuk wax that gives the wooden floor its mirror finish, but there are also the paraffin and methylated spirits used for the Tilley lamp, the heavy grease on the lever frame and rockers, the Brasso that keeps the description plates on the levers so bright, the smoke that leaks out of the ill-fitting pipe at the back of the stove and Mr. Bond's strong thick Twist tobacco.

As we drink our steaming hot tea from the chipped enamel tin mugs, Mr. Bond tells me about his life as a young boy, and how he joined L.M.S. as a lad porter and has done most jobs on the railway. Whenever he speaks to me about his work I am always left in no doubt that he is in his favourite vocation and that he is content with his lot.

For the first time in the school's history, pupil reports are issued. Mine is abysmal with a position of thirty second out of forty – Mrs Slaney's comment at the bottom is 'Harry can do better.' Also for the first time we have health checks. I am well below average height and weight, four feet seven inches and five stones and one pound. Another major change is the introduction of the eleven plus examination for entry to grammar schools. Twenty children out of one hundred pass the examination, and some are from the lower grades. One of these is Graham who passes to go to Wolstanton Grammar School. Jimmy Hanley passes to go to Newcastle High School. This has quite an effect on my young life. As well as missing the comradeship of these two pals, for the first time I feel the stigma of failure.

At eleven years old I am below average height and weight, have close cropped mousy-coloured hair with a fringe and a bit that sticks up at the back defying all attempts to beat it into submission with the back of the brush. I am quite shy in the presence of adults; terrified when left on my own in the house; brave to the point of foolhardiness with my peer group; a downright coward when wounded; deeply thoughtful when involved in my own world; academically poor; generous in nature; extremely sociable with those whom I feel at ease and have a developing wicked sense of humour that leads me into all sorts of scrapes, but also helps to see me through the next phase of my life.

CHAPTER NINE

PLAYING

• 1 •

At home the war's the main topic of conversation, but life goes on as though it was nothing more than a distant rumour. The wireless is always switched on for the news. Programmes are produced to give us all a lift. Tommy Handley's 'Itma' provides levity and fun, and 'Workers Playtime', a programme broadcast from factories predominantly involved in the war effort and transmitted live on the Light Programme during lunch times helps relieve the tension. The wireless is the focal point of our lives, particularly during the long, dark winter evenings. As a family, we gather round the fire to listen to our favourite programmes - P C 49 with Brian Reece, a weekly story about a London policeman, and the Paul Temple mysteries written by Francis Durbridge. Paul Temple is a crime writer and private investigator played by Peter Coke with his wife Steve, a Fleet Street journalist played by Marjorie Westbury. The theme tune for the series is Vivian Ellis' Coronation Scot, a tune that will forever symbolise these happy family times. Plays are serialised, each episode leaving us on the edge of our seats, desperate for next week's instalment. We never miss the boxing matches with commentators Raymond Glendenning and Eamonn Andrews. Our hero is Bruce Woodcock, the British heavyweight champion. 'Children's Hour' is broadcast in the late afternoon. It includes Larry the Lamb from Toytown. Uncle Mac and Aunty Violet present the show.

So, the wireless is only an attraction for occasional evening family entertainment with the exception, that is, of one programme, Dick Barton – Special Agent. At 6.45 p.m. the streets empty. "The Devil's War Gallop", signals the start of a fifteen minutes' weekday serial that attracts an entire generation of children to the wireless. Dick Barton, and his comrades in arms, Snowy and Jock, have a cult following. Never before have so many young ears been glued to the wireless sets. This is the age of the comic, where serialised heroes leave their young fans hanging in suspense and biting their finger nails to the bone until the next edition. The exploits of Dick Barton are the embodiment of this, and British youth revels in it, most listening to the omnibus one and a quarter hour repeat edition on Saturday mornings, and I am no exception. It runs from 1946 to 1951 and has such an impact that the establishment becomes concerned about the effect it might be having on fifteen million of the nation's young minds and decides to withdraw it. It's replaced by a weak circus story called "The Daring Dexter's" and ultimately by the long-running country soap opera, "The Archers".

• 2 •

Whatever the weather, I'm outside. There are three 'gathering points'. The gas lamp at the bottom of Orton Road, directly opposite to Graham's house, the pig bin outside Kenny Wright's in Orton Road and the railway bridge at the end of Albemarle Road. The gas lamp hasn't been lit up since the outbreak of the war, but it's a nice thing to hang around, discuss things, climb up and swing from. It's here that I learn about life, my friends and the news that is important to us. Community pig bins are for scraps of food to feed the local pigs - nothing is wasted. Everyone is encouraged to keep pigs to help with the war effort. Any bones in pig bins are sent from our area to Massey's Bone Works close to Silverdale Road, for the manufacture of glue. On warm summer days, if the wind is in the 'wrong' direction, the smell is pretty powerful. The pig bin also smells foul. Nevertheless, we use it as a wicket; a goal post; for parking our bikes; for climbing over garden fences to retrieve balls. It's 'den' when we play 'tick' and 'hide and seek', and the central point for discussing what we are going to do next! Sometimes we gather on the bridge over the brook. Generally the brook is just a steady flow and 'jumpable' in a number of places, but after heavy rain, as if forgetting its good behaviour, it turns into a raging torrent and, restricted by the tunnel under the railway, it backs up to cause serious flooding in the four fields. And if it is raining and there is no entry available, we use the railway bridge.

   A 'piece of jam', mixed cocoa and sugar, and pieces of bread ladled with dripping and sprinkled with salt keep the wolf from the door. Table salt is bought in lumps the size of a house brick. Dripping's either bought from the butcher, or scooped from the top of the gravy left over from Sunday's roast.

   Generally, we fair quite well for food with a hot meal most days and fresh meat three or four times a week. Breakfast's usually porridge or toast. Joan fetches the meat for both ourselves and neighbours from Percy Billington's as part of her 'errands'. Percy's butchers shop is in George Street, Newcastle, a good half hour's walk from home. Everyone has a chip pan. Chips are fried mainly in lard, sometimes dripping. On Sundays we have a cooked breakfast of bacon and eggs followed at dinnertime, around one o'clock, with a 'Sunday roast'. Almost everyone has a Sunday roast. The smell of the joints cooking pervades the entire neighbourhood. Together, with the freshness of newly washed linen, the tang of the sticks drying in the oven and the smoke from the tiny paraffin oil lamp in my bedroom when the wick is too high, are smells most associated with these times. Religiously, Dad sharpens the carving knife on a whetstone at the top of the garden and brings in a clump of fresh mint to be chopped. For tea we have a salad with the inevitable Spam or Prem, perhaps followed by jelly and a piece of home made cake if we are lucky. We all sit down together for meals. In spite of being a poor family, table manners are rigidly enforced. When a meal is finished we have to ask to leave the table.

• 4 •

Like most families there are times when we have our problems. We all have mumps and measles, and Joan and Mary catch scarlet fever. Our family doctors are Dr. Anderson and Dr. Mowatt and they pop in whenever they are passing to see how we all are.

Aged one, serious whooping cough; at four I have my tonsils out, just like having a tooth extracted, a quick squirt of gas, a painless snip and it's all over, then back home for some of Mrs Bird's red jelly, almost worth it as we only have jelly on Sunday and Christmas Day; when eleven, off school for three weeks with abscesses in my ears leaving both eardrums perforated and, apart from a few broken bones, nothing more serious. The major downside of illness is being confined to barracks. Friends soon discover if anyone has a problem and call round with comics to swap, and then the inevitable "read it, read it, read it" signals yet another disappointment.

When the girls skip and play with tops and whips, we boys play with bowlers and shotties. Only those boys with older sisters will know of the agonies and torment they wreak. I inevitably become the butt of the jokes, the excuse for their being late, the 'Oh, no! he'll hold us up.' I am blamed for all things, more often than not, deservedly so. In fairness, they have to help with the cleaning and polishing and all I have to do is to run errands and tear up the newspaper into squares and hang it on the nail in the lavatory – the Daily Herald is alright, but the print comes off the Evening Sentinel. My arms ache with holding skeins of wool while Joan and Mary busily roll it into balls. Whilst I play with my lead soldiers, they knit and crochet and make cork wool. They badger Dad to knock four tacks into a cotton spool and then they wrap the wool, hook it and pull it through the bottom of the spool. The corded wool is made into place mats and tea cosies. They make pompoms by threading wool through two milk bottle tops and when full, the wool is cut, the tops taken off and the pompoms fluffed out. And I can never get the hang of cat's cradles! They also make shopping bags with milk bottle tops. The tops are made of waxed paper with a pouring hole in the centre. They collect them for months and wrap them individually with raffia, finally tying them all together, bag-shape, and fit two raffia handles. When they play teacher, I am their pupil. I can knit and read before going to school.

My two sisters are as alike as chalk and cheese. Joan, older by nineteen months is thin and has dark hair. She has a strong character and lots of energy, serious minded and old for her years. Mary is fair and bonny and takes life as it

A Staffordshire Lad

comes. She is giggly and funny and irresponsible. Both have dark brown, deep-set eyes like Mum.

• 5 •

Devoid of any adult concerns, wartime is a pretty exciting time for most of us. We don't go hungry and our general health is good. We have our own wars. We re-enact the films we see. Cowboys and Indians; Robin Hood and his Merry Men – the 1938 film with Errol Flynn, the definitive 'Robin' – the arguments as to who is to be Robin; the acceptance of being either Will Scarlett or Little John; the reluctance to be Friar Tuck; the enthusiasm to make bows and arrows.

Christmas times are very special in spite of the austerity brought about by the war. The run up to Christmas is a time for making decorations, mincemeat and money. We spend hours making paper chains out of coloured tissue and crepe paper. There are also sheets of aluminium paper that appear from somewhere that we fold into concertina shaped chains. We all chip in when making the mincemeat. The dried fruit, sent in one of the food parcels by Aunty Rachael who lives in Australia, the suet, carrots, apples and sugar are weighed and put into basins. I turn the handle on the mincer while the girls feed the ingredients into the hopper. We all make a wish as each of us gives the mincemeat a stir before Mum ladles it into jars. Mum makes the puddings weeks before and stores them in the pantry. Carol singing is a way of making a few bob and is looked forward to with eager anticipation. Swathed in coats and gloves and hats, and with a candle in a jar, we set off in groups of five at the most, clever enough to know that more would reduce the spoils, and, through trial and error, we know those homes that hold the generous types and those that don't.

On Christmas Eve our thick, black, woolly stockings are hung up expectantly on the end of the bed head. Santa Claus is never too generous, but he does his best, and to be honest, we never expect too much. Until I am ten, all my Christmases are wartime ones. What we never have, we never pine for. We always have the traditional threepenny bit, an apple and a bag of something, supplemented with books and homemade toys. What can't be bought is often made. As a result of the war, people have become very resourceful and innovative as money and products are in short supply. Rag dolls and knitwear are popular, as are wooden items such as the rocking parrot, the monkey up a stick, tops and whips and skipping ropes. Joan and Mary are given miniature wooden stool moneyboxes with a secret access underneath. I have a wheelbarrow. My first Christmas of the war is also my best in terms of gifts. Dad wins a Hornby clockwork model railway set in a raffle. It is complete with engine, tender, trucks and track. I also have a tin double-decker London bus and a clockwork tank with rubber tracks that reverses when it bumps into anything solid. These toys are the mainstay of my enjoyment throughout the early years of the war. It is hard for parents having to watch their children grow up and being unable to indulge them with even a Christmas tree. As if to compensate for these lean years, I am given a football, a pair of football boots, darts and a dartboard for the Christmas after the war. It is about this time that Mary spills the beans about Santa Claus, and even then I have to ask Mum to confirm it. Well, who drinks the glass of port wine and eats the mince pie that is left in the hearth, then?

Christmas Days are so memorable. Dad, up early to light the fire and cook the bird; Mum, preparing the vegetables and setting the table and the Christmas Day carol service on the wireless, the predictable "We saw three ships come

A Staffordshire Lad

sailing in." The cards, the presents, the warmth inside, the cold outside, a hundred different smells in the kitchen, the friendly arguments as to who should have a leg, the steaming pudding as the piece of old sheet is taken off, the feeling of appetites replete, the settling down in front of the fire to listen to the King's speech and special seasonal programmes on the wireless, the feelings of satisfaction and the contentment and simple joy of the day expressed on the faces of the three of us smiling children and our mum and dad, no doubt, considering their good fortune for those few moments of respite amidst the terror of war that is raging just a few hundred miles away.

Just after Christmas, Mum takes us to the pantomime at the Theatre Royal, Hanley. We queue for hours in all weathers before winding our way up the many flights of stairs to the 'Gods'. I secretly envy the posh kids in the boxes and ache to chuck my apple core at them.

Spring is heralded by the lady's smocks that we gather by the armfuls from the marsh meadows, followed by the annual trek to the bluebell wood at Keele Hall. The Easter holiday is the first big break from school since Christmas and is an opportunity to get rid of the winter blues and pent up energy.

Summer is the time I help Percy Johnson make hay in the fields opposite our house, and later, dig there for pig nuts. Going to the cattle auction at Newcastle Smithfield, wearing wellies and carrying a stick to poke the animals and chase them in and out of the pens, before and after the sales.

Autumn is exciting when the conkers are encouraged to fall with a well-aimed stick and battles royal take place in the back yard. The number of victories depends on how long the conker has been soaked in vinegar, or baked in the oven. And the number of red knuckles depends upon the accuracy of the opponent's aim. Gathering blackberries by the bowlful. Carrying them home with red-stained fingers and tongues, to be stewed with a few fallen Bramleys supplied by a good neighbour, and consumed with lashings of Bird's custard after Sunday dinner. Gathering firewood for the bonfire, saving up to buy fireworks from Walter Ward's hardware shop in Silverdale. Gathering in Donald Cowburn's garden on bonfire night, waving goodbye to the Guy who'd helped to swell the fireworks' fund, baggsing the burnt out fireworks, roasting the spuds and eating them, half raw, with good helpings of salt, black hands and smarting lips.

Winter is the time for slides down Hassam Avenue, sledging in Percy's fields and snowballing just about everywhere. Cold fingers, wet gloves, ruddy cheeks and chilblained toes. Making winter warmers with old tin cans pierced all over with a six-inch nail and stuffed with old rags, suspended on a length of wire and set alight, then swung around at a rate of knots to keep it burning. Warming gloved hands on the can and getting asphyxiated by the obnoxious fumes emanating from it.

Cowboys and Indians are popular. Deciding who is to be who is always emotive. Roles identified, the 'wild west' erupts with the two opposing foes whooping and hooting and banging like a pack of Banshees, slapping backsides with right hands, holding imaginary reins with the left, skipping and running around the block, envying those who have replica colt 45 and matching holsters. Then the arguments as to who or who isn't dead, and who will or will not lie down. Comparing notes; the discussions; the whys and wherefores, until the next time.

Sundays to chapel, twice sometimes three times. Dad is 'chapel reared'. He has strong Victorian principles – he believes that children should be brought up in the way of the Lord and to him that means Wesleyan Methodism. The chapel is situated in Liverpool Road at the top of King Street. It imbeds strong, Christian values. To me it means missing out on time with my friends. Star cards marked; Sunday School Treats - visits to Trentham Park, or parties at Knutton Institute; the annual anniversary; 'walking round'; stories with meaning; the beatitudes; the Ten Commandments; the creeds; 'Sunny Smiles' pictures and envelopes for subscriptions to help orphan children; traditional hymns. There is always a downside and some events are not looked forward to with much enthusiasm. The 'chapel anniversary' is one. This comprises two events. On a summer Sunday we do 'the walk'. How I hate this? The congregation assembles at the chapel and then we walk, in procession, along a prescribed route, stopping every so often to sing a hymn whilst senior members carried out a door-to-door collection to boost chapel funds; most embarrassing when we stop near to home and I can see all my mates pointing and laughing at me. Later in the summer we have to go 'on stage'. For weeks we practise for the anniversary-singing concert ready to go 'on stage'. This is a temporary tiered platform built at the front of the chapel. All the girls wear their anniversary frocks and the lads are in their Sunday best. For Methodists, this is the event of the year, and the chapel is always heaving, with extra seats placed in the aisles. In spite of it keeping me away from the serious business of 'playing out', I quite enjoy the singing, especially Handel's Largo with the words from 'Come Gladsome Spring'.

I never had a birthday party. In fact birthdays, at least mine, are almost non-events. My seventh birthday is memorable because I have a proper birthday card with a large seven on it. Previously my cards have been postcards with a simple greeting on the front. I only go to one birthday party and that is to Jimmy Hanley's tenth. I don't know what to expect and my naiveté is plainly evident, because after the jelly and blancmange, I am the one who is rolled up in the carpet, and have my face painted with soot.

I join the chapel cubs for a while, and later the scouts. I don't learn much, but I enjoy the tracking. Mary and I transfer our allegiance from chapel to St. Michael's Church of England, a brand new church in St. Michael's Road, Cross Heath. Mary becomes a Sunday school teacher and I join the choir. I enjoy the one year that I am in the choir. It teaches me the value of good music and harmony. I don't think the black cassocks have ever been cleaned, but our mums wash our surplices once a week, and for their pains, we are invited to the annual day out to Llandudno. At thirteen, I lie about by age and joined 435 Squadron Air Training Corps at Cross Heath barracks.

Later in my teens I join the newly formed Bignall-End Male Voice choir. It is led by Billy Bowers, renowned locally for his musical talent and his shining baldhead. The choir becomes quite well known and gives concerts. At one of the concerts Ada Allsop, a much-esteemed classical singer of the day, accompanies us.

As a family we only have one holiday together. Not long after the war Uncle Harry loans us his caravan at Stratford-upon-Avon for a week. Uncle Harry has helped a local farmer develop a caravan site in one of his fields adjacent to the River Avon. It is called Avon Park and is now one of the biggest in the area. They create a lido on a bend in the river where we all go swimming, that is, with the exception of Mum. It's the only time I ever see Dad in a swimming costume. He borrows Uncle Harry's black leotard-style swimsuit which accentuates his roundness. He bobs up and down like a float on a fishing line. I almost split my sides when I see him, but diplomatically, wait until I am on my own before I let go. I sleep in a tent by the side of the 'van and became very friendly with the boy next door. He has a kayak and spends the first weekend teaching me how to use it. He returns home on Sunday evening, but leaves the kayak for me to use during the week. When Joan and Mary are out looking for boys, I am competing with the rapids. Every day I am on the river and occasionally paddle down to Stratford, about a mile away, to do Mum's errands.

We had been to Avon Park the previous year when we were visiting Uncle Harry and Aunty Annie at their home in Shirley. Uncle Harry had a large white van and piled us all in together with some of his neighbours' children for a day by the river. It was this visit that whetted Dad's appetite for our holiday the following year.

Then there is the camping, no doubt inspired by 'Just William'. In the 1947 summer holidays Graham, Brian and I decide to 'go camping'. It takes a lot of planning but eventually the three of us, with a paraphernalia of pots, pans and methylated spirit stoves strapped to us, and looking like a tinkers sons' convention, and with Brian's dog Timmy on a piece of string trotting reluctantly behind, set off for Springwood, a small hamlet between Chesterton and Wood Lane. Graham's uncle, ten times removed, lives in one of the cottages and allows us to pitch our tent in his field. This is our big adventure, our window of independence, surviving against the odds and living off the land. The truth is that we are totally ill-prepared; have insufficient food; nothing for the dog; cold and uncomfortable at night and stung by wasps during the day. And, during the first night, we are attacked by a spooked horse that rips the guy ropes off the tent collapsing it on top of us The following day we are attacked by some local roughs who ransack the tent and break some of the dishes including a jug loaned to us by 'Uncle' for holding the water. We arrive home after the third day dirty, dishevelled and ravenous. Amazingly, with the fortitude, or the foolhardiness of youth, we go again the following year. This time without Brian who is on holiday in the Isle of Man with his family, so we borrow Timmy, without their knowledge, who is being cared for by Mrs Hall, their next door neighbour. With a wealth of experience from the previous year, we fair about the same, without the traumas of the horse and vandals, but still pleased to get home to a decent meal.

Trolleys and scooters, whistles and hooters;
Rusty old bikes, long summer hikes;
Bowling with tyres, building bonfires;
Letting off bangers, dropping some clangers;
Swinging from trees, skinning our knees;
Running and jumping, slapping and thumping;
New foreign stamps, annual camps;
Games of French cricket, a bin for the wicket;
Tag and Sly Fox, drying our socks;
Hiding and hunting, puffing and grunting;
Flying a kite, picking a fight;
Old comic swapping, hop scotch hopping;
Carol singing, nettle stinging;
Stealing a ride, making a slide;
Multiple skipping, coloured top whipping; Climbing and falling, laughing and bawling;
Aching for snowfalls, and making snowballs;
Freezing red nose, chilblains on toes;
Baggsing and shouting, bragging and scouting;
Happy and glad, lonely and sad;
Teasing the dogs, dipping for frogs;
Postman's knock, running the block;
Dinky cars and playing on bars;
Jumping the brook, sharing a book;

A Staffordshire Lad

Country lane tramping, ill equipped camping;
Staying out late, Dad at the gate;
Fencing and shooting, whooping and hooting;
Shotties and jacks, climbing haystacks;
Goin' apple scrumpin', then home for a thumpin';
Blackberry picking and rhubarb nicking;
Afternoon flicks, all sorts of tricks;
Short cuts to town, then Johnny Mack Brown;
Goodies and baddies, funnies and saddies;
Jolly pictures and dolly mixtures;
Stan and Ollie, Lassie the collie;
Charlie Chan, Sabu and Tarzan.

CHAPTER TEN

WALKING

• 1 •

I suppose everyone has a memory tucked away of some special event in their lives that seems to be of a time when everything came together to provide fun or laughter or some kind of unique enjoyment, at least I like to think so. I'd never heard of Butterton. For all I knew it could have been on the other side of the moon. Yet this delightfully rural out-of-the-way village, just less than three miles south west of Newcastle, sticks out as the place where I had one of those extra specially happy days.

Butterton nestles between the hamlets of The Lymes, Shutlanehead and Millstone Green, the latter its former name, and is just to the west of the busy M6 and Junction Fifteen, although motorways weren't even an evil glint in the planner's eye at the time I am about to relate.

I had been to Butterton once before, but wasn't aware of it at the time. In my last year at Hassell Street I'd become friendly with John Hamilton whose father was a professional naturalist and, as is often the case, the father's interest rubbed off on the son. Mrs Slaney's stories had sparked an awareness in Nature in all of us and one Saturday morning in the last week of May 1946 a group of about ten of us gathered outside the town hall in Newcastle to catch the Market Drayton bus. Armed with notebooks and pencils we went as far as Two Mile Lane and for the next four hours walked the lanes around what I later discovered to be Butterton, a tiny hamlet surrounded by isolated farms and served by St. Thomas' Anglican Church. The church is unusual for both its conical tower and its position which is at the end of a long lane and set on the edge of a wood. Sometimes referred to as 'The Church in the Wood', it is joined to the village by a public footpath. It was built in the Neo-Norman style in 1845 and was designed by a Mr Hopper of London.

For the first time in my life I became aware of the multitude of wild flowers that grew in our countryside. It was an awakening that aroused a lifetime interest for me. John knew them all, taught us the names and showed us how to press them in our books. The lanes were heavy with the perfume of May blossom; cow parsley; jack-by-the-hedge; red campion; bluebells just starting to fade; the polished faces of buttercup; dandelions both golden flowers and misty seed heads; blue bird's eye; bird's foot trefoil; gorse; cranes bill; lady smock; wild sedge; knot wort; pignut fern; red sorrel; ragged robin; and cowslip. Acutely aware of Mrs Slaney's warning about picking wild flowers, John showed us how to pinch out the blooms without damaging the bulbs.

Other than John, I can't remember any of the others who accompanied us. I am only conscious of a feeling of warm companionship, light-heartedness and laughter whenever I think of that time.

A Staffordshire Lad

Today I caught a waft of May, from exactly where, it's hard to say,
And then I saw across the way, beyond a field of new mown hay,
A hawthorn swathed in purest white, hoary blossom, reflecting light
As scattered snow so fresh and bright rests on a hedge at winter's height.
Fragrance borne on gentle breeze, drifted through adjacent trees
And then continued by degrees, until it almost seemed to seize
My psyche, awakening forgotten joys of walks down lanes with girls and boys,
Of blithe and fun-filled childish noise that only carefree youth enjoys.
Too soon the reverie was gone. Of scented zephyr there was none
Just memories to reflect upon and youth-filled times to ponder on.

• 2 •

The following year proved to be one of those magical summers that seem to go on for ever. The sort that you can almost believe were responsible for having us believe that summers were so much better then. Perhaps the biggest influence on walking was Mr Johnson, Brian's father. He was a small, mild-mannered, quietly spoken, cheerful man. He worked as an engineer at Meaford Power Station. I remember him with affection, interested in all things 'boyish' and, regardless of the weather, always seeming to wear a floppy old trilby and a grubby, belted, mid-wars' 'Mac'. He was the personification of 'the man' in the Rupert Bear stories. He was a remarkably unremarkable man, if that's not too much of a paradox. Remarkable in that he spent most of his leisure time entertaining Brian, his only child; dads just didn't do that in those days. He introduced us to the Apedale canal, a stretch of the unused waterway that had been so instrumental in transporting raw material and finished goods from the adjacent Apedale Iron Works. This firm was part of the Stanier empire, the largest iron company in North Staffordshire. In 1890 it was taken over by the Midland Company and closed in 1930. The massive redundant plant lay about the decaying yard as a memorial to the once thriving industry, robbed of its life-giving raw material and thus its investment and ultimate profit. And, no doubt, like the men who sweated out a living there, bewailing those days when the factory throbbed and roared at the height of its production. It now forms part of the Apedale Heritage Museum at Chesterton.

Like the plant, the canal had also outlived its usefulness and many parts were returning back to natural landscape as Mother Nature wills. To get to the canal we had to walk through the Brymbo. The coalmine workshops lay adjacent to the iron works. Mr Johnson had discovered a long, narrow entry between two of the workshops, providing a short cut to the canal. It was about fifty yards long and just wide enough for one person to pass through at a time. It was dark, eerie, smelly and disconcertingly scary, but it was worth it because the canal was a haven for sticklebacks, red penks, newts and frogspawn. In spite of all we caught, carried home in jam jars with string handles, there were always plenty left for our next visits.

Mr Johnson did things that children liked. In his quiet way, he entertained them, enjoyed the results and chuckled along with them. One day he came home with an old three-wheeled Victorian bath chair that was to become the highlight of our pleasure and fun for the following twelve months.

It was one hot August day and Graham and I were wiling away the hours in the garden. We'd played ourselves out. We'd burst all the tar bubbles in the road; worn the tyres off our Dinky cars; repaired our catapults with the new square elastic from Hanley market and freshly cut tongues from a pair of my dad's shoes; had two pieces of jam and a glass of Tizer; examined Graham's new four-way spoke spanner in detail, and discussed every possible angle to make a few bob. The Johnson's had gone on holiday. Mrs Johnson's sister had a farm at Butterton. They had an old 1920's bus converted into temporary living accommodation. It was here that they spent their holidays. We heard a car pull up outside Brian's house and went to have a look. It was Mr Johnson. He'd come back in a taxi to collect Graham, me and the old bath chair to take us to play with Brian at the farm.

Not that we did anything significant, more that it was a day just filled with fun. The weather was perfect. We played with the old bath chair till our backs ached with pushing and our sides with laughing; taking turns to give each other rides around the lovely country lanes, occasionally stopping at the spring to quench our thirsts. We'd lie on our stomachs, push away the wild watercress and lap up the icy cold water. We dragged the old chair out of ditches, crashed it into hedges, navigated it through herds of cows, we did everything to it that the manufacturer had designed against and claimed could never happen. It was the nearest to a rally car any invalid chair ever came.

We scrumped apples from Auntie's orchard and hid in a ditch to scoff them until our bellies ached and then, were caught in the act of going for seconds.

During the afternoon Brian's cousin Julia joined us and we played in the old hay barn. The barn was half filled with loose hay and we helter-skeltered from top to bottom, the old place shaking with childish laughter. We pushed and jumped and fell about demented. We were hot and sweaty and smelled of the musty, rankness of dried hay and corn dust.

It was late evening before the taxi came to take us home. They all waved us off, Mr Johnson still chuckling at the fun we'd had and, no doubt, blessing the day he'd found that old bath chair on the tip in Lower Street. We sat in the back totally drained yet with a feeling that we'd had such a good time.

I am still haunted by the happiness of that special day and recall it with fondness. The war was over. Things were retuning to some form of normality. The world was beckoning. It was a good place to be and a good time to be living in. Often, since that long-ago day, I have wondered why it is that such a simple time has remained with me in photographic detail. Perhaps, because it marked a threshold in some way; I was moving subconsciously from childhood to adolescence; stepping from being cared for to taking more responsibility for myself.

CHAPTER ELEVEN

HOLIDAYING

• 1 •

I could never pass over my boyhood without mentioning my Uncle Harry. Outside of my immediate family, he had the biggest influence on me and is the one person I miss most, even now, in spite of it being more than forty years since his death.

He had a single-minded, independent streak that helped forge his future. He was nothing if not positive and optimistic in all things. His strength of character and magnetic personality outshone and dominated. Wherever he went, his presence abounded. He was a big man, not over tall, about six feet, but solid, square-backed, powerful, yet he had an overwhelming gentleness often rare in strong character. He also had humility, sympathy and empathy for others. He had the light of mischief in his large blue eyes that seemed to liquidise if he felt he'd caused offence. He was devoted to his family. Although lacking in education, he was intelligent and blessed with an inordinate amount of common sense.

A Staffordshire Lad

He was generous to a fault, but the characteristic that is foremost in my memory was his extraordinary self-confidence.

William Harry Tomkinson was born on 13 April 1898, the second son and eleven years older than my mother. It seemed his character had been moulded in the womb. His free-spiritedness was of constant concern to his mother. She was confounded by the varying excuses for his truancy and concerned with his impatience to be 'grown up'. After running away at sixteen to enlist at the outbreak of the Great War and returned home post haste, he eventually signed on in the Royal Artillery in April 1915. He was a born survivor. Because of his youth, he was pushed to the back of the queue when his regiment embarked on the troopship to France and had to wait for another. The first ship was lost with all on board. For such a big man, he was extremely light on his feet and held ballroom dancing classes with his sister Beattie in the large room at the Crewe Arms.

He had a ruddy complexion that smacked of good food, good living and the open air. The corners of his eyes were wrinkled with laughter lines and his smile was exaggerated somehow by the genetic missing tooth in the left side of the upper row. His deep bass voice resonated and boomed when he laughed which was often. His fists were round, strong, solid and dependable.

Uncle Harry and Aunty Annie were our rich relations; they worked hard for what they had. After the Great War Uncle Harry went to Canada and joined the Canadian Police in Saskatchewan. It was a tough life, having responsibility for hundreds of square miles. He once told me that in the depths of winter with temperatures of more than forty degrees below freezing, he'd lie in bed and watch the frost creep ever closer to the red hot glowing stove and feel the blankets stiffen as hard as boards. Aunty Annie, was only a teenager, when she went out to him, but the severe weather affected her health forcing them both to return home.

Back in England, he had various jobs including a road-building ganger in charge of a wild bunch of Irish navvies. It was whilst building a new road in Lower Street, Newcastle, that he cut through an underground passage leading from St. Giles church to John O' Gaunt's castle on the Silverdale Road. The passage was sealed at one end with a three feet thick oak door. Many artefacts were discovered. Uncle Harry managed to get a piece of the wooden doorway for the landlord of a nearby pub in exchange for his first free pint whenever he called in. The landlord had a couple of candlesticks turned out of it and a brass label screwed to the base to tell the story.

Later, Uncle Harry and Aunty Annie moved from their Biddulph home to Birmingham where Uncle Harry bought a lorry and moved into haulage. He had an eye for an opportunity. New parks were opening; football pitches required annual refurbishment and housing developments were breeding like flies. Grass seeding was labour intensive and long winded. The instant lawn had arrived and Uncle Harry made sure he was in at the ground level, so to speak! He became very successful and was the main contractor for the Birmingham City, Aston Villa and West Bromwich Albion football clubs. Initially the turf was cut by hand using a flat, pointed spade, folded and loaded on to the lorry. Later, Uncle Harry bought machines that did all the operations automatically, and branched out into selling a comprehensive range of garden supplies to the general public.

His dress sense verged on the flamboyant. He wore large, floppy trilby hats cocked at a rakish angle; outrageous ties sporting the Windsor knot on which he'd splash a dash of 'Carnation Poppy' or 'Devonshire Violets' scent scrounged

A Staffordshire Lad

from one of his sisters; a thick, unbuttoned Dhobi overcoat; a red spotted yellow Sammy scarf; quite often a fresh flower in his lapel; light check trousers; heavy brown brogues; a tartan car rug on his left arm to catch the hairs from the ever-moulting Chang, his Pekinese lap dog.

He was no less showy in his choice of cars. He had them not to impress, but just because he liked them. His first love was a large Indian motorbike and sidecar and his first car was an open top, three-wheeler B.S.A. sports model that reeked of leather. I used to sit in the Dickey seat, the envy of my mates, and was taken on spins to Ivy Cottage and Biddulph, Aunty Annie's family home. His next car was a massive, grey, American Studebaker, the first American car to be seen in the neighbourhood and more suited to Uncle Harry's size and style. A black Humber Imperial, the epitome of luxury, followed this, and then a series of Sunbeam Talbots, chosen because of their success in international rallies.

• 2 •

When he came to see us, I'd sit with my sisters totally captivated listening to his latest bits of news and imploring him to tell us a story about his colourful life. Wreathed in smiles, he'd conjure something up, heavily embroidered with his own brand of mischief and fun and stretching the truth increasingly as he wound our excitement up to fever pitch: "When I emigrated for Canada, my shipmate was a lad from Uttoxeter who was blessed with a double row of teeth and used them as a weapon with great effect when an irate Swedish café owner attacked us with a meat cleaver for having no money to pay the bill. He clamped the man's arm with his teeth forcing him to drop the cleaver." We loved to hear the tales of when he was a boy. "My first job after leaving school was stable boy at the 'big house'. One of the horses I looked after was a feisty young steed that lashed out with his hind legs whenever I was within striking distance. One day, after a particularly vicious kick, I could take no more and rammed a pitchfork smartly into the animal's hindquarters."

Occasionally we'd have family 'get together' at home and after tea the uncles would keep us entertained. We were all introduced to 'Kissing the Blarney Stone'. Everyone was kept in the kitchen and one by one we were blindfolded and led into the living room by Uncle Charlie who explained that we were going to kiss the Blarney Stone. We had to kneel down, bend forward and kiss something warm and very hairy. The blindfold was taken off and the first thing we saw was Uncle Reg's rear end disappearing into his trousers. Disgust turned into hilarity when the next victim was brought in and we realised that the Blarney Stone was not part of Uncle Reg's unmentionable anatomy, but Uncle Harry's large, hairy forearms.

Uncle Harry was a very generous man. He just wanted everyone to enjoy life to the full and share a little in his good fortune. On every visit he gave Joan a half crown piece to be shared between the three of us. Ten old pennies each, a crock of gold to children who had grown to know the value of money and the ways it could work. At Christmas time he'd dress up as Santa Claus and give every kid in the neighbourhood a gift from a large bag placed at the bottom of his garden. Granddad Sam also made a perfect Santa when he stayed over for Christmas.

During my early teens I accompanied Granddad Sam to Uncle Harry's for two weeks of my summer holidays. I'd meet him off the bus in Newcastle and we'd catch the Hanley bus outside Henry White's. A bus to Birmingham completed the journey in two and a half hours. These were precious

A Staffordshire Lad

times when Granddad would tell me all manner of things, especially his love and experiences of his life in the pit. He was fascinated with massive engineering plant, especially the huge head gear wheels, a pair of which at Cannock always drew comment. Uncle Harry would meet us at Digbeth bus depot and whisk us home for one of Auntie Annie's special roast dinners.

Every day was planned with a sort of informal forethought, but it's the days Uncle Harry and I spent together that are my fondest memories. While Granddad relaxed in the beautiful garden, it was business as usual for Uncle Harry. We'd set off in one of his lorries to negotiate deals for turf with Warwickshire farmers; to sites where turf was being cut and distributed; to banks and places of business at Stratford-upon-Avon and Warwick; to Henley for one of its well-known ice-creams; to garages to arrange repair or to collect vehicles. Sitting at the side of this happy, smiling, chuckling, joking giant of a man who'd go the wrong way around roundabouts for the sheer hell of it, was total bliss. He'd lean back in his seat and let me do the steering. One day we took a lorry to a garage at Dudley for work on the differential. While the job was being done we went to Dudley Zoo, caught a bus into Birmingham, had dinner at the Imperial, one of the city's largest hotels, waved to cousin Tony who was window cleaning Birmingham's highest building, went to see the Sunbeam Talbot that had recently won the Le Mans twenty four hours' race, then returned to collect the lorry and wound our way home for dinner.

• 3 •

The back garden of Uncle Harry's home at Colebrook Croft, Shirley, opened up into a large piece of ground converted into a full size bowling-green and croquet lawn with a figure eight shaped pool complete with a wooden bridge over it and a summerhouse alongside. He called it his 'little bit of England'. I liked to help him feed the pigs and hens and water the plants in the greenhouse.

Uncle Harry was always trying to get me teamed up with Margaret Freeman, the girl next-door, either to get me some company of my own age, or to satisfy his own wicked sense of humour. Apart from being quite shy of girls, I was perfectly happy to spend my time with him. However, to satisfy his requests, and his insatiable wickedness, I plucked up enough courage to ask Margaret to go to the pictures with me. Auntie Annie, ignorant of all of this, arranged for me to go to Llandudno with Uncle Wilf on the day in question and so, the date never came off. From that day Uncle Harry never mentioned Margaret to me again. I guess he'd had a serious talking to!

Uncle Harry had always kept two or three pigs. During rationing, when a pig was killed, the owners kept half and the government took the other half. Someone 'shopped' Uncle Harry one day when one of his pigs was killed and he found a policemen climbing through a hole in the hedge. He told Uncle Harry that he'd heard a pig had been killed and had come to investigate. Uncle Harry told him he had no right to force his way through the hedge and sent him round to the front door, about five minutes walk. This gave Uncle Harry time to hide the dead pig in the compost heap.

My last stay occurred when I was eighteen. I had completed my initial training in the R.A.F. and was on a week's embarkation leave. Towards the end of the week I rang Uncle Harry and asked if I could spend the weekend with him. I left early on Saturday morning 15th February 1955 knowing that I was kicking the dust of home from my boots, probably forever. A beaming Uncle Harry met me off the train as though I was his long lost son. Our handshake transmitted warmth and mutual affection, unaware that this would be the last occasion we'd share one of our very special times together. At least, I was unaware, but throughout my life, whenever I have remembered that day, I have wondered whether he had some suspicion and, as a consequence, arranged the sort of day that only he could conjure up.

Writing about this period of my life has caused me to step back, reflect and paradoxically, share with myself these times that were so special to me when I was a boy. It's as though I'm actually living rather than re-living them. Yet not living, more like being present as an observer. As the fog of these boyhood days evaporates, and the light of memory spreads through my being, I am first filled with the warmth of recognition and then with the pleasure of being reunited with my dear uncle.

His Sunbeam Talbot was parked in a restricted area defying anyone and everyone to question its authority. He navigated his way through the narrow streets re-writing the Highway Code and ignoring the irate horns of other cars with chuckles and comments like "He's got good brakes." We pulled into a vacant space in the Bull Ring. It was alive with street performers, fire-eaters, Indians lying on beds of nails and every kind of spiv flogging everything imaginable. Uncle Harry bought a pack of 'Gillette' razor blades for a fraction of the normal price only to find out later that there was only one blade and four pieces of cardboard in the 'pack'. He thought it was a great joke and admired anyone who could pull one over him.

From there we went to the sports stadium and met Alex Griffiths, the famous Birmingham boxing promoter. Clearly he and Uncle Harry, who had been a boxer in his youth, were good friends. He invited us into the weighing room just in time to see Randolph Turpin, the ex-world middleweight champion and his latest opponent, Ray Schmitt, 'the Luxemburg Terror', weighing in for their match later that day. There was none of the eyeballing, intimidating antics used by today's boxers, just a friendly handshake and an exchange of best wishes for a good, clean match, followed by the usual press photographs.

We hurried back to Aunty Annie who by some miracle had waved her magic wand to produce one of her spectacular dinners on cue just as we walked through the door. No communication necessary. Just the knowledge acquired through a lifetime's experience and trust in her man's reliability that he would not let her down.

With our bellies full and the delightful combination of kitchen smells necessary to produce such a meal still tickling our noses, we set off again. First we called at the yard to pick up Uncle Harry's foreman and it was there I was told that we were going to see the FA fourth round cup tie at the Hawthorns between Doncaster Rovers and Aston Villa. Uncle Harry had the contracts to re-turf the Birmingham City, Aston Villa and West Bromwich Albion's football pitches. He had a scarf for each, but could never remember the different club's colours, so he kept all three in the boot of his car. It took a little while to convince him that he needed to wear the Villa's claret and blue, and to keep his head down if he saw any of West Bromwich's management.

The teams were so closely matched that this was the fourth replay. We had seats in the stand. I'd never had the luxury of sitting down at a football match before. It was a thrilling game. Doncaster Rovers were fielding their 'child prodigy', a sixteen-year-old genius called Alick Jeffery. The result was a 3-1 win for Doncaster. Dixon scored the Villa goal. Alec Jeffery scored two and Geoff Walker scored one for Doncaster.

After the game we hurried back to Aunty Annie who once again came up trumps with the catering. After tea we set off again. This time we picked up my cousin Brenda, the eldest of Uncle Wilf's daughters. Uncle Harry had secured us seats for the boxing match. It was typical of him to provide some company for me of my own age as he had a ringside seat booked. We sat at the back straining our eyes to see the fight, which was stopped in round eight to prevent Schmitt receiving further punishment. A young Joe Erskine, who was later to become British heavyweight champion, was also on the bill.

The next morning I lay in bed longer than was my custom and spent a little while reflecting on my stays in that spare room over the last few years. This was the same room where Felix had practised freefall through the window, landing uninjured on the old couch in the conservatory and leaving a cat-shaped hole in the glass roof. It was the room where I pretended to be ill when Aunty Annie wanted me to go on a bus trip with Uncle Wilf and I wanted to keep my date to go to the pictures with Margaret Freeman from next door. And it was in here that, reputedly, Uncle Harry had hidden a pile of his money from intruders and the taxman protected by eighteen stones of bone and muscle and the biggest double-barrelled shotgun I'd ever seen. This same room where a couple of flitches of salt bacon were hung from huge hooks in the ceiling, and off which, like on this particular morning, a couple of thick slices had been cut, the appetising smell pervading the whole house, playing havoc with my taste buds and willing me to get up and get stuck in.

All too soon it was time to leave what I had come to know as my second home. Uncle Harry took me to the station, my kit bag on my shoulder and Chang, in his usual place, on top of a blanket on Uncle Harry's left arm. We didn't talk much. Everything had been aired. He just said "So long; take care; drop me a line when you're settled in." The carriage door was slammed shut as if closing a distinctive chapter on my life. As the train pulled out, the steam and smoke from the engine enveloped him, isolating him from the others on the platform. I think of him still in the image of that day, the true hero of my early life exuding self-reliance and confidence. And yet, there was something else, a look of sadness with a faraway, distant expression.

I have often wondered if his mind had been transported back forty years or so to the time when he was in uniform and about my age and leaving home. Was he reminded of the wanton horror of the Great War with its destruction of the flower of a generation of young men, the total waste of humanity, and the good fortune that brought him and his three brothers safely home? Maybe he thought of the time he saw his eldest brother in the distance who had walked many miles from the front just to find him. Perhaps it was thoughts like these that inspired in him such a feeling of 'family'. As I sat alone on the train I made up my mind that throughout my life I would try to emulate his example and hopefully, give back to him in his later life some of the pleasure that he had given to me and to the rest of his family. Regrettably, he died in February 1963, just before his sixty-fifth birthday, and so denying me the opportunity of paying back some of the debt I owe him. I will be eternally grateful for his life, a life that was lived to the full.

A Staffordshire Lad

My mother and sisters, Joan and Mary at 30 Albermarle Road

Ivy Cottage

A Staffordshire Lad

My Grandfather Sam (centre) with sons Wilf, Harry, Reg and Albert.

My mother at 18 years of age.

My Father at 18 years of age.

A Staffordshire Lad

My grandfather, Sam Tomkinson.

My grandmother, Lucy Tomkinson.

A Staffordshire Lad

The three Tomkinson sisters, Ruth Beattie and my mother, Dorothy.

My Parents' wedding reception (left to right, back row) Auntie Ruth, My Grandparents Arthur and Mary Titley, and my grandparents Sam and Lucy Tomkinson..

A Staffordshire Lad

By comparison with other areas Newcastle suffered very little by way of bomb damage in the last war. The havoc caused to individual homes was still considerable as this photograph of Taylor Avenue, May Bank (1941) depicts.

Bombed out houses at May Bank (Wolstanton).

Holditch Colliery 'The Brymbo'.

A Staffordshire Lad

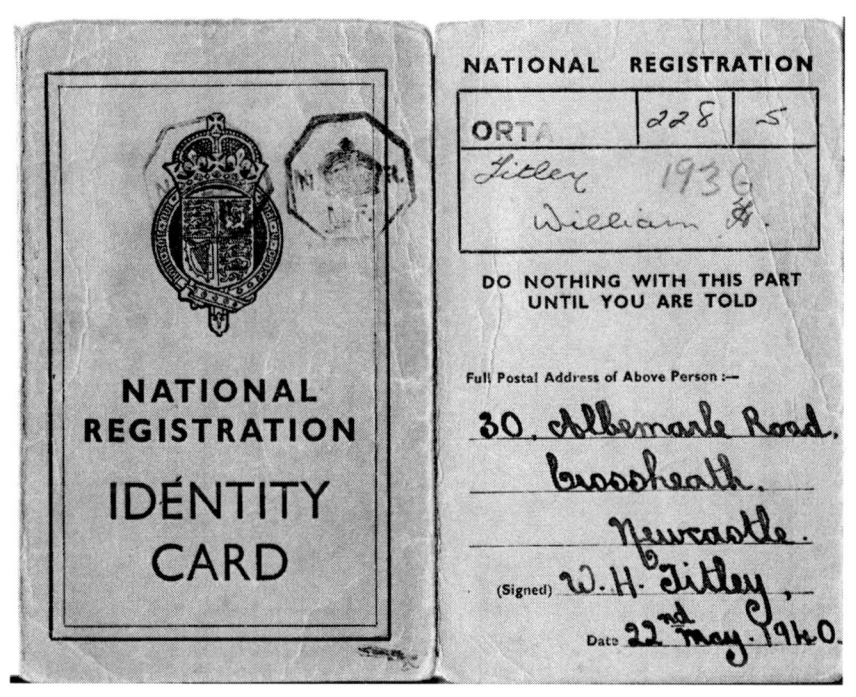

My identity card

Leycett Pit (Madeley Colliery)

A Staffordshire Lad

Ryecroft School

Hassell Street School Staff, (centre seated) Mr. Showan, Headmaster, Mrs. Slaney second from right.

A Staffordshire Lad

Uncle Harry, Auntie Annie and Chang with evacuees Sylvia and Pearl.

Orme Boys School

A Staffordshire Lad

Orme Boys School staff (front row, left to right) Mrs Gassick, Dr Adams, headmaster, centre.

Myself (front) digging the foundations for the greenhouse.

Myself as 'The Genie'
(centre with Turban.)

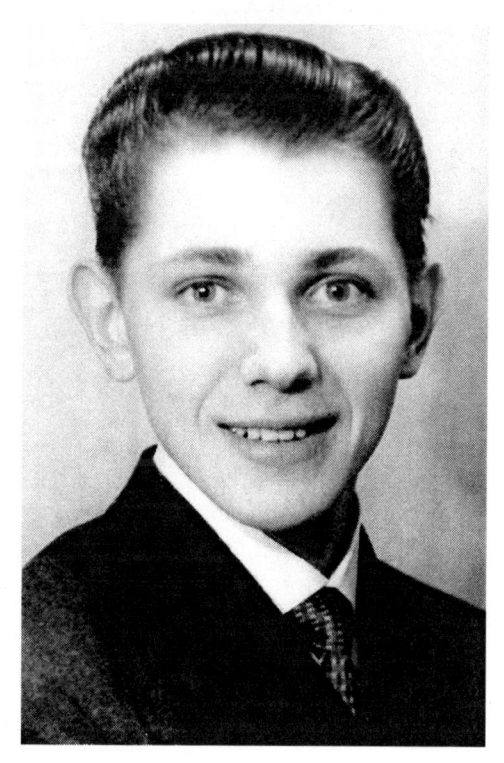

Myself at 18 years of age.

A Staffordshire Lad

(From left to right) Myself with Graham Stanton and Graham Roberts.

Newcastle High School from Mount Pleasant circa 1874.

A Staffordshire Lad

Newcastle High School staff, 1952 (centre seated) Mr JM Todd, (centre back row) Albert Miles.

Lower VI, (seated left to right), Peter Anderson, John France Myself, 'Rags' Riley and Albert Miles.

111

A Staffordshire Lad

Uncle Harry at 18 years of age.

Myself at Square Bashing Camp, West Kirby, 1954.

A Staffordshire Lad

Myself (back row, right) Germany 1955.

Myself (extreme right) at a Demob Party in Germany.

A Staffordshire Lad

Colonel Trares receiving my report at Wahn, Germany in 2007.

CHAPTER TWELVE

LEARNING - ORME BOYS SCHOOL

• 1 •

So, in September 1947, with much trepidation, I wound my way through the back lanes to the Orme Boys County Secondary Modern School at Pool Dam.

The school had been built in 1851 when there were still ships, laden with convicts, sailing on eight-month voyages to Australia. It was built on the site of a prison at a cost of £1,870. It was described as 'affording no less than eight square feet per boy'. The ethos of the school embraced the regulations introduced when the first Orme School, or English School, was founded in 1704:

'With respect to the Master: that he be capable of, and diligent in teaching, to read, write and cast accounts; that he be honest and virtuous and sober (in) conversation. With respect to the boys: that they can at least spell well; that they are competently well habited according to their parents circumstances, but all kept very clean'. During the reorganisation of education in Newcastle in 1872 when the Orme Girls and Newcastle High School were built on each side of Stubbs Walks, the Orme School became the Middle School. The Orme was constructed of large, red sandstone blocks with a round tower on one side and sited on the corners of Orme Road, Pool Dam and the Higherland.

I was fortunate to still have a few of my Hassell Street pals with me like Brian Tinsley, Ray Evans, Geoffrey Allman, Jimmy Ryalls and Graham Amphlett, but we were also joined with boys from other schools, mainly Friarswood, in particular, Eddie Humpage, Frank Shufflebottom, Eric Pullin, Len Cooper, Gabby Redfern, Stuart Prendergast and Tom Johnson, the latter, who by a peculiar twist of fate, became the only contact with the Orme that I kept into old age. Even as I write, almost sixty years on, Tom is lying in a hospital bed waiting for a heart by-pass that hopefully will extend his life and our long friendship. Coincidentally, whilst we were getting acquainted, two young girls were doing the same at an infants school in Trent Vale just a couple of miles away who were destined to become lifelong friends and our respective wives. Long associations like ours where our lives have been inextricably linked with a series of strange coincidences, make it harder to come to terms when serious illness and tragedy strikes. Two other boys that became very good friends were Peter Dobson and Selwyn Howell. I was to be at the Orme for two very happy years.

I was placed in 1A with an unpopular teacher called Norman Lowe. He had his favourites. Unfortunately, Tom was not one of them and was later transferred to the B stream, mainly as a result of being absent for a long spell with a very serious bout of pneumonia. Whether it was the disappointment of losing my friends who had passed their scholarship, or a new school with new friends, new teachers and a fresh approach that ignited some latent intellect, or that I was developing some sense of responsibility, or maybe a combination of all of these factors that contributed to produce an improvement in my academic progress, is pure speculation. The fact is that at the end of the first year I dragged myself up to second in the class. It was a great year for me. For the first time since starting to school I looked forward with eager anticipation to every lesson.

• 2 •

The day began with morning assembly. Our headmaster, Dr. Adams, was a man who demanded respect. He retired in 1948. As well as advocating a Christian start to the day, he passed on little pearls of wisdom that held me in good stead for many years. He was extremely fit and started each day with a cold shower. I was introduced to some new subjects as well as having to contend with some of the boring old ones. Mr Turner was our music teacher. He could have been a parson if looks had been primary qualifications. He had thin, fair hair, a scrubbed, shiny face with a benign sort of 'peace to all men' look permanently set on his face. His eyes were blue and, directed by a classic 'parson's nose', continuously searched for the great beyond somewhere above our heads at some obscure point at the back of the classroom. However, what he taught, stuck. He introduced us to the masters and gave us an appreciation of technical aspects such as harmonisation and control. He also took us for gardening. The school had a small vegetable plot on the opposite side of Keele Road. Should we not remember to bring our old shoes on gardening days, we'd risk a hell fire and brimstone sermon from him and be consigned to some mundane task

A Staffordshire Lad

inside. Mr Turner, a man of infinite musical know-how, was as deft with a garden fork as he was with a tuning fork, a rare combination of talents. Bad weather always seemed to know when it was our turn in the garden, but whatever it threw at us, I was in my element and became quite adept at sewing potatoes, first digging the trench, then laying in the muck, a layer of soil, then the seed eighteen inches apart, filling in and later, as the young shoots appeared, 'earthing up'. We also helped to put the base in for the greenhouse, the framework being built in carpentry workshop.

A new dimension for us was science. The Orme boys had a large laboratory. Our master was Jackie Pallister, a mild-mannered, quiet and reserved character. He was quietly spoken yet dynamic with demonstrations and experiments. He totally absorbed my attention filling my head with chemical, physical and biological wonders and allowing us to prove the theories with practical experiments. The Bunsen burner. Oh! the Bunsen burner. Intense concentration brought about the loss of an eyebrow and reduction in my fringe. Yet, if ever I was going to shine, it was under his guidance. I came top in science at the end of the first year. Another favourite subject was craft studies - woodwork and metalwork. Mr Micklewright took us for metalwork and Mr. Martin for woodwork. I loved the workshop. It had a unique smell of fish glue, resin, stain, French polish, sawdust and freshly planed wood chippings. I had found my vocation. I had an affinity with wood. I was going to be a carpenter. Initially we made simple items such as pencil racks and pipe holders, later graduating to more difficult exercises using dovetail, and mortise and tenon joints. However, as things turned out, it was Tom who became a highly skilled pattern maker, running his own successful business until he retired.

A Staffordshire Lad

English has always been a special subject for me and my interest and knowledge expanded under the guidance of our formidable teacher, Mrs. 'Ma' Gassick. She was large. Her enormous form draped over her stool like Zeus on the mountain, unmoving for the duration of each lesson. She had deep set, humourless eyes with dark, heavy bags beneath. She was a disciplinarian, instructing by fear and I mopped it up. She gained my immediate respect when she told us about her friendship with Mitchell, the designer of the Spitfire, and lost it one day when she sat on an inkwell. Tom Johnson had the unenviable and embarrassing job of cleaning the ink off the back of her extra large bloomers whilst the rest of us looked on with boyish amusement.

Our history teacher was Mr Singer. He looked like a character out of a Victorian novel. His hair was long, and curly, and his clothes were tweedy, a cross between Sir Walter Raleigh and Sherlock Holmes.

Maths was the subject I liked least of all. The maths master was Poppa Cooke, a dour, elderly man with no sense of humour. His favourite expression was 'by means of a trick', and I was certainly baffled by the wizardry of algebra. Mental arithmetic and geometry I could cope with, but simultaneous and quadratic equations left me cold.

Our sports teacher was Len Williams who lived in Roberts Avenue. He played football for the local team and later became sports teacher at my next school. I had already developed a taste for sport at Hassell Street and revelled in the increased and well-organised activities. The school was well endowed with footballing talent. Two of our lads, Peter Proctor and Don Ratcliffe became professional footballers with Stoke City. The school also won the 1951-52 cup final, Tom was in the team, although this was some time after I'd left. Football was well organised with training and competition. I never shone at the sport, but enjoyed the physical aspect, the challenge and the competitiveness of the game. However, athletics was my first love and, in spite of being small, I was able to hold my own on the running track and in the field events with achievements at the 1949 annual athletics sports day. We used to compete in shorts and pumps displaying our undernourished tin ribs to all the world. We were also taken to the swimming baths although my progress came to an abrupt stop in January 1949 when both of my ears were perforated as a result of abscesses.

• 3 •

The late 1940's was an era for screen classics such as David Lean's productions of Charles Dickens' 'Oliver Twist' and 'Great Expectations'. The school took us to see them and encouraged questions and comment afterwards. We were also taken to London to see the damage caused by the blitz. We assembled at Newcastle railway station early one cold winter morning, to board the special train. We were given a large brown parcel label on which our names were written. Mum was a bit concerned about my going because I was just getting over my ear problem. However, I was fine and kept myself amused playing my new mouth organ. I had seen pictures of the war damage in the newspapers and on the cinema newsreels, but I wasn't prepared for the scale of the devastation that existed in London. Entire buildings and streets were just piles of rubble, but there was also a great deal of activity involved in the rebuilding programme. We spent the afternoon at Whipsnade, my very first visit to a zoo. It was the first time I'd travelled on the train from New-castle. Railway stations always had a certain fascination for me. Graham, Brian and myself would spend hours on the bridge in King Street looking at the comings and goings of the L.M.S trains and the activity in the adjoining goods yard of Newcastle station. It was here we saw the first 'mechanical horse', a maroon three wheeled tractor replacing the old cart-horses - progress indeed! The station, built in 1852, was one of the first opened by the North Staffordshire Railway (The Knotty). The goods yard was built on the bed of an old canal. Newcastle was linked to Stoke station through a long tunnel that passed under nearby Basford. Westward, the line joined Silverdale, Keele, Madeley, Pipe Gate, Norton-in-Hales and Market Drayton. Later passenger sidings were introduced at Liverpool Road and at the Brampton level crossings, and it was here that our neighbour Mr Bond, who later became Lord Mayor of Newcastle, used to show me the workings of his signal box on my way home from school.

My first Christmas at the Orme was pretty exciting. The nativity play boasted a host of angels, and Brian Tinsley, Len Cooper and myself, being the three smallest boys in the school, all altos, were chosen to sing one of the carols, roles that we were never allowed to forget either by the staff, or by the boys. I was also given the lead role in the Christmas play 'The Genie and the Lamp', and was word perfect well before the big night. I really looked the part complete with turban, robes and make-up. I climbed the step ladder in the wings, leapt onto the stage at the correct cue amidst a tremendous flash and bang, surprising me, the gunpowder plotters and the audience so much I completely forgot my lines. It caused a few laughs and Mum and Dad enjoyed themselves. This was the only event Dad ever came to; perhaps this was the reason why! The final act of the evening was also memorable. The hall lights were turned off and one of the senior boys, John Osborne, came through the main door holding an old fashioned coach lamp and followed by 'the three kings'. He

A Staffordshire Lad

sang the old carol "We three kings of orient are.." in an almost ethereal voice as he walked round the hall. It was the first time I'd heard the carol and has since remained special to me.

In the spring of 1948, some of us were invited to take the application examinations to the Technical College and the thirteen plus for entry to one of the grammar schools. The Ministry of Education had realised that some children developed later than others, and a few places were made available to accommodate them. The examination for the technical college was taken at Burslem. I have very little knowledge of the day, just a feeling that it was the last place on earth I wanted to go to. My luck held. I failed.

On the contrary, my day at Newcastle High School was great. The impressive edifice surrounded by acres of sports fields reminded me of Greyfriars and the Billy Bunter stories. Geoffrey Allman and I were the only Orme boys offered the thirteen plus examination. We sat the papers with about fifteen other nominations on the stage in the large, impressive assembly hall. I became friendly with a boy called Peter Mainwaring, son of the family that owned the local bus company. He was only interested in boxing and didn't view the event at all seriously. I never saw him again.

A few weeks later we had gathered in our classes in the school playground on a warm summer Thursday afternoon and Dr. Adams came out to make an announcement. Much to our embarrassment, he asked Geoffrey Allman and myself to join him at the front. He informed the entire school how proud he was that two of his pupils had passed their scholarships and at the end of term would be leaving prior to starting at Newcastle High School in September. After offering us his congratulations, he said that it was an achievement not only for us, but also for the school, and reflected the high standard of education provided by the staff at the Orme Boys. Many times his words have come to mind, and I have pondered just how many of the boys we were shortly to leave behind, justified the same opportunity that we had been given. And later, when I was able to assess the academic merit and intellect of my new classmates, I realised that the lottery for deciding who should and who should not have a grammar school education, left a lot to be desired.

• 4 •

Clearly, the Orme had shaken me out of my sleepy attitude towards education, and had provided me with a springboard to higher educational opportunities. In later years I was sorry that I hadn't felt any sadness at leaving, overwhelmed as I was by the excitement of this new challenge and adventure, and I am embarrassed that I was sixty-six before I visited the Orme again. On 9th December 2002, Tom Johnson and I went to re-visit the old school. The original buildings are now grade two listed, but the function of it has completed changed. It ceased to provide secondary education in 1966 and then provided a multi-discipline education that catered for adult training, day nursery, victim support and leisure.

I didn't hang about getting home on the day my scholarship was announced. I had a single-minded mission. It was Thursday, Dad's half day, and I wanted to know if he would stick to his promise and buy me a new bike for passing. I found him trudging up the lane wearing his old grey velour trilby, his gardening clothes and his wellies, and pushing a barrow-load of soil for planting out his geraniums. He was pleased with my news and readily agreed to the new bike, but I have often wondered at the other thoughts that would have crowded his mind. We didn't have any money and there would have to be a very big outlay to send me to the new school. As a callous and inconsiderate youth, such thoughts were far from my mind, but I had more than one pang of conscience when I discovered that Mum had to sacrifice her life at home and take a job in a factory so that the costs could be met. From that moment I was determined that any money I was able to earn would go straight into Mum's pocket.

CHAPTER THIRTEEN

EARNING

• 1 •

Money was always in very short supply and, as a consequence, I developed a profound respect for it. Pocket money hadn't been invented. Wartime, more than any other, was a time of austerity, sharing with family, friends and neighbours; helping one another and running errands with no thought of reward, in spite of the odd surprises. But on those infrequent occasions when a few coppers came our way, it was exciting and exhilarating. My share of the half a crown given by Uncle Harry, whenever he visited, put ten pennies in my pocket and, not only gave me a lot of purchasing power, but also taught me the value and importance of having money. Money was a means of getting the things that I wanted, and if I was to have any, it was clear to me then that I'd have to earn it, and earning it was hard work, not least as on this occasion:

I screwed up one eye and peeped, rather nervously, with the other through a gap in the weather-beaten, board fencing. The fence formed a barrier between the cobbled entry of the dismal alleyway and the yard where the handcarts were stored. It would have been so much easier to have simply walked through the open gate, but I hadn't the nerve; the owner was known to eat lads like me for breakfast and my overactive mind only served to exaggerate the myth. It had taken a lot of courage to get this far, but the situation was desperate and I had no choice.

I was about ten or eleven at the time. I had a small round face dominated by two enormous blue eyes, short-cropped, mousey coloured hair with a fringe that fell over my eyebrows, and knee-length grey socks that fell over my ankles exposing a colourful array of cuts and bruises. I was wearing a faded green jumper, out at the elbows, and short grey trousers that would have been out at the back but for two large patches.

The yard was filled with handcarts of various sizes each brightly painted and having its own unique design. Some had pictures of wild animals and flowers; others had scrolls and complicated patterns in a kind of Romany style; all were tilted on their tail-ends to allow the rain to run off. A dilapidated shed stood in one corner of the yard and scrawled on the door in white chalk was the cost of hire per hour 'sixpence small, nine-pence large'. At the front of the shed, a brazier punched out of a rusty oil drum, crackled and glowed to a cherry red. A pile of coke, half covered by a worn and dirty tarpaulin, was placed conveniently by.

The shed door opened and a grizzly-haired rascal of a man appeared. He wore an oversized, unbuttoned army greatcoat tied around the middle with a piece of coarse string; a pair of colourless boots stuck out beneath leather gaiters and his greasy hair played host, not least, to an oily cloth cap moulded through incessant use to the shape of his large head. Indeed, the man's appearance was in direct contrast to his carts in that they were bright and cheerful and he was not. At last I forced my trembling legs in the general direction of the gate and then into the yard. The noise of my tips and studs on the cobbles caused the man to look up, "What's they want," he mumbled? His vocabulary was limited and followed by a series of grunts. Eventually, after much muttering, a hire was agreed. I handed over the two three-penny bits from my hot, sticky little hand, the proceeds from the dandelion and burdock bottles I'd taken back to Polly's corner shop. "Pick thee sen one ite from yon littleuns," the man grunted, "an' mek sure theet back in an 'our." I was instantly attracted to a green and yellow cart covered in clusters of pink roses. There were seven blooms in each cluster, just like Dad's 'Seven Sisters' climbing rose on the trellis at home.

I wheeled it out of the yard. As soon as I was beyond shouting distance, I set off at a lick through the High Street, over the 'stones', down Lower Street where the cart nearly ran away from me, and then into the gas works. My worst fear was realised. A large queue all waiting for the same thing – coke! The unwanted bi-product from processing coal gas was given away free of charge and, because of coal-rationing, there was a big demand. A few folk had hired carts similar to mine, but the rest had a variety of old prams, orange-box trolleys, wheelbarrows and even an old bath chair.

As I waited, I reflected on the need to keep the fire going at home. As far as I was concerned, the war had gone on for ever; I'd never known peacetime, at least not that I could remember. All I knew was that it had brought many hardships, not least the rationing, and the allocation of coal did not provide enough to keep the fire going. The current hard winter had stretched our ration of one bag of coal a week to the very limit and, for much of the time, like many others, we'd struggled to manage. I'd overheard Dad telling Mum that there was nothing more downright miserable and soul-destroying than staring into the back of a fireless grate on a bitterly cold winter's night. I was old enough to understand that our very existence depended on the fire. It heated all the water for washing the family and their clothes; it cooked the food; dried the rain-soaked clothes; thawed chilblained hands and feet; heated the bricks that aired the beds; and it drew us together in a family circle where we could forget the cold at our backs by concentrating on the cheery ruddy glow emanating at our fronts.

Before the last shovel-full of coal and bucketful of slack had been used up, I'd seen the worried look on Dad's face struggling to come to terms with what to do next. Both of my granddads were miners and received their special allowance of coal that was in excess of their personal needs, and both had offered to help out. Unfortunately, they each lived five miles away and the problem was transportation. One day after work , Dad decided to catch the bus to Granddad Sam's. He filled a sack with a half hundredweight of coal, dragged it to the bus stop a couple of hundred yards away, pleaded with the bus conductor to let him put it under the stairs and, when he arrived, I met him with one of the girl's bikes for the big push up the back lanes to home.

Dad and I also spent a few Sunday mornings 'picking coal' at the local pit. We rode to the Brymbo pit on our bikes and picked the waste pieces of coal off the tip. It had been pretty dangerous work as the mine was still being worked. The waste material from the mine was hauled up the tip by a massive container on an incline railway. At the top it would rotate, throwing its load of rocks and slag out onto the tip. When picking, we had to keep one eye on the container and, when it was half way up, scatter in all directions with the rest of the pickers to avoid being buried under the slag. The full sacks were hauled back on our bikes. It had been hard and hazardous work, but the coal we'd picked had been good and helped to keep the fire going.

During the spring and summer months, Dad had scoured the fields and lanes for broken branches and stored them in the chicken run at the top of the garden to dry out. Later, he'd spent an hour or so each weekend sawing them into logs on the trestle made for the purpose. I used to hold one end steady while Dad sawed them up. Dad had been offered the use of a neighbour's circular saw, and when I asked him why he hadn't accepted it, he said "hand-sawn logs burn longer!"

At last, my cart was filled. I knew I was late. I heard the clock in the tower of St. Giles' church strike the quarter past. I ran all the way up the back lane. Earlier, I'd negotiated with Mrs. Hall, one of our neighbours, to sell the load for a shilling, hence making one hundred per cent profit. After delivering it, I ran back to the yard, still within the hour; a round journey of about three miles. I paid the man another tanner and made another trip, this time for my dad, and I still had sixpence for another load later in the week.

I carried on fetching coke throughout that bitter winter. I always used the 'Seven Sisters' handcart. Now and again I was disappointed to discover that it was out on hire to someone else, but I'd patiently wait for it to come in, sometimes for as much as two hours. The coke I'd hauled supplemented the family's meagre ration of coal to the point that, with careful management, Dad never had to 'stare into a fireless grate' again.

Almost sixty years on, as I sit recalling these boyhood memories, return to the normality of the day, luxuriate in the comfort of total insulation from the elements, saturated in the wrap-around warmth of central heating, I can't help but feel a strange sadness; a kind of grief not only for my lost self, but for the time when families, friends and neighbours pulled together to overcome the privations and difficulties thrust upon them by uncontrollable forces.

• 2 •

There were a couple of exceptions when Lady Luck smiled on me. The first was on the annual pilgrimage to Pat Collins' fair during Wakes Week, traditionally held on the site of the auction at Newcastle. In spite of having nothing to spend, there was enough interest just walking round the side shows. Boxing booths; the fattest woman and the smallest man in the world; the coconut shies; shooting galleries; roll-a-penny stalls; the swing boats; the cake walk; the carousel; massive steam generators to supply the electricity for the rides, lighting and piped music; the screams; the noise; the candy floss; toffee apples and brandy snap; the slot machines bursting with money and programmed to release only a small fraction so as to whet the appetites of passers by and encourage them to part with yet another penny. Pressing all the levers on the slot machines annoyed the attendant and satisfied our mischief. It was on one of these that I noticed a silver ball just waiting to be shot round the track. I pressed the lever and was delighted to see the ball enter the 'win' hole. Back came the ball and out popped a penny. The next time I tried, it went into the 'lose' hole, but to my surprise the ball returned. Every time I played a 'lose' the ball came back, and every time I played a 'win' the ball came back and I won a penny. I went home delighted with my trouser pockets stretching down to my knees.

The second time was when Graham and I noticed something shining on the grass outside Normier Tyres at the top of Roberts Avenue. It was a two-shilling piece. Then we found half-a-crown, some other silver and some copper. We'd struck gold. The only times we ever saw so much silver was when the gas meter was emptied.

We tried selling horse manure for tuppence a bucket until the supply ran out. We made kites with coloured tissue paper from Woolworth's, and three-foot canes and balls of string from Garner's garden shop in Newcastle. We spent hours with flour paste and scissors making all sorts of shaped kites from simple triangular to complex, hexagonal with an outer fringe. The difficult part was tying in the 'balliols'. These were the three strings that were tied equidistant from the top half outer edges to maintain the kite in flight at the correct angle, and to reduce rocking. The tail was tied to the two bottom points and weighted the kite to stop it ducking and diving. We only sold one! And the firewood enterprise was not much more successful.

• 3 •

I soon came to realise that running errands wasn't going to make me rich. I quite willingly ran errands for Mum and Dad as my small share of the weekly chores. On Saturday mornings I'd take the wireless accumulator to be charged at Sheila Lawton's in Liverpool Road, returning with the freshly charged one, and in winter I'd get our weekly pint of paraffin for the Valor stove we kept in the bathroom, and bedside lamps from the same place. Mine was blue and the girls' was red. Dad's Littlewood's football coupon had to be posted on Thursday to get there in time. I followed his instructions to the letter not wanting to be the cause of his losing the jackpot. I had to kiss the stamp and then rub the envelope on my behind before I popped it into the pillar-box on the corner of Kimberly Road. In spite of my ignorance and embarrassment, I performed the act out of sight behind the pillar-box. Evidently, I didn't get it right because he never won a penny. I learned that by putting a "no thank you" expression on my face when asked to run an errand usually brought some return. I was beginning to learn not to be taken for granted.

Uncle Harry once bet me three pence that I couldn't run round his bowling green with a large potato in my mouth in one minute. I did it in less, but he never knew. He was laughing so much he forgot to look at his watch. Aged thirteen, I had a paper round at Walter Tryner's newsagent at the top of Roberts Avenue. I delivered morning papers and Evening Sentinels as well Sunday papers, all for ten bob a week. Every penny I earned from this point on, I gave to Mum who had started to work to keep me at school. I was given half-a-crown each week for pocket money. Whilst I had yearned for little, there were attractions that I would have had if money had been available. When I was eight Joan had been given a copy of the monthly paperback, Sunny Stories, and passed it on to me. I became entranced in the lives of elves and pixies and read the print off them. I must have subconsciously craved for more of the same, but we were never bought comics and periodicals. The desire for more must have lay dormant because, when I was an 'affluent' teenager, I bought one and although I never admitted it to anyone, enjoyed it. I used to be fascinated whenever I passed the British Restaurant in Newcastle on my way to the library. It was the first time I'd seen communal eating on such a large scale. Sure enough when I had a couple of bob to spare, in I went and sampled the fare. I was quite impressed.

The following year, after school, for three afternoons and fifteen bob a week , I delivered meat for Percy Billington, our butchers in George Street near Hartshill. I made the deliveries on an old tradesman's bike with a very large basket on the front; tough going, as most of the customers lived in the area that included the notorious Hartshill and Basford banks. When I'd finished the deliveries, I helped in the shop making sausages and cleaning down. The sausages were made using two large bowls of breadcrumbs to one of minced meat, the unwanted scraps from the day's sales. These were mixed and fed into the hopper of the machine and the intestine skin was fitted onto the nozzle. As the handle was turned with the right hand, the sausage meat was forced into the skin. The left hand was used to twist the sausage every six inches to make the links.

For two weeks of the Christmas holiday in 1950 and 1951, I worked on the Christmas post. Our neighbour, Mr Finneron, got me the job. My half cousin and classmate, John Bate, whose father was also a postman, shared the Chesterton run with me. Getting up early wasn't a problem and I was always at the Newcastle Post Office sorting room way before the required time of 6.00 a.m. The post van dropped us off at The Hollows in Chesterton, a thriving mining community. I delivered to the houses on the left side of the main road and John did the right. My first call was Loomer Road where my cousin Doreen lived with husband Len and their three children Lynne, Janis and Paul. Joan, Mary and I were Godparents to each of them respectively. A warm welcome and a nice cup of tea were always on the cards.

I was often soaked to the skin, blue with cold, chased by dogs and terrified by geese, but I just loved posting letters. It was a simple, uncomplicated job, and the friendly mining folk, coupled with the warmth of the Christmas Spirit, made it enjoyable. Considering the poverty in the area, the people were very generous, and where a 'Christmas Box' could not be afforded, there was a mince pie, a hot drink spiced with something seasonal, or just a friendly greeting. This was particularly so on Christmas morning, the last delivery, when often I was invited into people's homes to share a glass of sherry. The worst part was having to complete a complicated time sheet that included shift allowance, overtime and expenses. Each year I earned about twelve pounds and about five pounds in tips, well above the average weekly pay. Perhaps the easiest and most lucrative job I had was as an observer during the 1953 Road Census. We had just gone to live in Bignall End and Uncle George, who worked on the council, got me the job. Initially, I had to cycle to the Council Offices in Stone for my instructions and census forms. My observation point was outside a farm at Balterley, near Audley. I shared the two shifts 6.00 a. m. –2.00 p. m. and 2.00 p. m. – 10 p.m. with a man who lived in Wereton. We had to record all vehicles of each type that passed the observation point. The Nantwich Road in those days was not much more than a country lane and the most difficult part was staying awake. On bad days the farmer's wife let me sit in the dairy adjacent to the road. At the end of the two weeks I cycled back to Stone to hand in my forms and collect my wages. I didn't know how much I'd earned until I arrived home and was overjoyed to discover that it was twenty-two pounds.

Not all my part time jobs were so easy. The hardest work I had, and for the least pay, was also during the summer holidays of 1953. I offered to help Peter Carter with the haymaking. Peter was a farmer who lived opposite to us in Diglake Street. He was a quiet, unsociable man with a hunter's face, florid and mean. He wore a hacking jacket, flat cap pulled over his eyes, knee-length leather leggings and hard-tipped boots. He kept a number of horses to work the land and to pull his trap. We worked from dawn to dusk, initially turning the new-mown hay with rakes to dry it out. When dry, we stacked it into mini-stacks using pitchforks. Later we pitched the hay onto the cart. Finally, the hay was stacked in the barn. During quieter moments Peter would send me into the garden to gather soft fruits for his wife. At the end of the week he gave me two half crown pieces. Never were any of his willing horses flogged as much as I was during that week. But at seventeen I was very fit. Anything physical was a challenge to my fitness, and in certain circumstances I'd have probably worked for nothing, but certainly not for such a mean old scrounger as he was.

However, my part time work had taught me that I wasn't afraid of hard work and indeed, thrived on it. It also taught me that to get anything I wanted, I first had to earn the money to buy it. I also learnt that there were people in the world who didn't subscribe to the rule of a fair day's pay for a fair day's work. The power of the pound helped to sharpen my wits and I never missed an opportunity to earn money.

CHAPTER FOURTEEN

BIKING

• 1 •

Probably top of the list of outside interests was biking. It had the biggest single influence on my young life and probably Graham's too. We cut our teeth on those Mickey Mouse tricycles with pedals on the front wheels when we were two years old. Then we both had black tricycles with chains and solid tyres before we went to school. Joan taught me to ride her two-wheeler when I was eight and from then on I was flying.

For the most part, the limit of our world was the distance our legs could carry us. Our bikes were passports to new horizons. They were not only an independent means of travel to unknown destinations, but they also opened up an interest in mechanical engineering. They had bits and pieces that just asked to be stripped down and reassembled.

We got to know every nut, bolt, washer, ball bearing, cotter pin, crank and sprocket ratio, cable, brakes, grease nipple, stem, forks, spoke and handle bars' adjustment. We could shorten chains, repair punctures and fit almost anything from bells to brake blocks, from saddles to mudguards. We knew all the places to get spare parts and all the tricks for cheap and easy repairs. At the outset, I borrowed my sisters' bikes, and occasionally Dad's.

Dad promised me a new bike if I passed my scholarship, so when I failed the eleven plus, my disappointment may have been greater than his, only compensated for when I passed the thirteen plus. He sent me to Stan Lowe, a cousin of his who kept a bike shop at Bignall-End. I knew exactly what I wanted. It was an all gold Hercules racer with derailleur gears. It was the only motivation I had for going to Diglake Street. Forever fearful that it would be sold, I never missed an opportunity to visit Stan's shop. It was always there just waiting to be lifted out and given to me. It was made for me. I knew every inch of it even before I had it. I could hardly contain myself when the big day arrived to collect it. Stan and Arthur Evans, another of Dad's cousins, were getting it ready for me in the workshop at the back of the shop. The place reeked with a delightful mixture of rubber solution, tyres and machine oil. All the advice and instructions went straight over the top of my head – I just couldn't wait to get out and on it. And when I did, I was on a magic carpet. I was flying at last.

Graham and I used to cycle far and wide and Whitmore Common was a favourite place of ours, the best part of a twenty miles round trip. If you're still out there Graham, can you remember the time when your tyre punctured on Whitmore common and we started for home with you on my saddle and you holding on to your bike at the same time? Then we flagged down a van driver. It turned out to be Eric Fletcher's dad. He made us swear that we hadn't just let the tyre down to get a free ride. For an instant, I thought he was going to make me ride home on my own, but our luck held and he delivered us to the top of Hassam Avenue.

Can you also remember taking me to Rudyard Lake, Mow Cop and the Harecastle tunnel? We also often biked to Trentham to watch the steam traction lorries hauling the heavy armoured tanks from the Stafford factory to the docks at Liverpool. They often stopped there to fill up with water from the river Trent. We'd fly down Porthill Bank; no hands down Bignall Hill; broadsides on the frozen pond at Scott Hay; race down Black Bank and Milehouse Lane, along the fields by the brook to home.

Sometimes we'd share a bike; crossbars, handlebars as well as saddles turned it into dual transport. Yet all of this was so fleeting, just a few years before we moved to motorcycles.

• 2 •

We became very interested in the fast growing sport of cycle speedway. The sport became popular at the height of the motorcycle speedway craze of the late forties. On Saturday nights we went to see Stoke Potters at Sun Street stadium. We'd wear our dad's shoes to make us feel grown up, immediately transforming us into men. We swaggered our way into the stadium believing that all twenty thousand fans that used to fill the all-standing concrete terraces were aware that we were no longer just kids. We knew all the technical jargon and we lived all the action. We had found our vocation. We were going to be speedway riders. The 'pushers' would start the bikes by pushing both bikes and riders. The J.A.P. (J A Prestwick) engines were revved up to full throttle, belching out exhaust fumes from the high-octane fuel and filling the air with their distinctive smell. When the tape went up the bikes would leap forward at seventy M.P.H. along the straight like bucking broncos. The bikes had no brakes and the engines were up to 500 cc. On the bends, the rider laid the bike over at a tremendous angle dragging the toe of the inside boot along the track into a long broadside and spraying cinders over a wide area. The atmosphere was electric. Ken Adams was captain, but our favourite rider was Gil Blake who, in one season scored maximum points at six consecutive meetings. The front wheels never touched the ground for the first fifty yards or so of each race. In one race, Gil overcooked his 'wheelie' and injured himself rather badly. After this he was never able to recover his form. Reg Fearman, Les Jenkins and Ray Harris were also amongst our favourites.

Cycle speedway was very popular locally with organised leagues. The dirt tracks were carved out on any bit of spare land. We made our own in the fields below Albemarle Road. Graham and I spent hours in the local scrap yards dismantling spare parts for our speedway bikes. They had to be very low-geared. This meant experimenting with a range of cranks and sprockets to get the right ratio. To get full strength from our thigh muscles, the rear end of the crossbar had to be lowered and re-welded to get the saddle as low as possible, and the handles high so that all the energy was directed onto the rear wheel. Philips produced a commercial bike, too expensive for us, but it gave us lots of good ideas. I rode a few times for the Stoke Stars team based by the canal in Etruria.

The longest cycle trip I made was when I was sixteen, just after we'd moved to Bignall-End. Graham 'Tuff' Bloor, a pal of mine from school, suggested we cycle to Rhyl in North Wales, during the summer holidays. We set off early in the morning and arrived at Rhyl about 2.00 p.m. We had about an hour walking along the sea front, bought a couple of sticks of rock to prove we'd made it and then started on the journey back. It was dark when we arrived home, very tired, but elated at our achievement of having completed the round trip of one hundred and fifty miles with hardly any breaks.

Graham left school at sixteen and became an indentured apprentice at the English Electric Company in Stafford, incidentally where, ultimately, I was to spend all my working life. He was given a 350 cc. Matchless motorbike in order to complete the eighteen mile journey. Graham was a natural and took to it like a duck to water. I was never happier than when I was sitting behind him on the pillion seat. We'd race up the Ironmarket, the deep-throated engine resonating as we passed between the Municipal Hall and the Post Office, our hair flying, eyes streaming, and hoping some girls we knew would see us. It was the nearest thing to being airborne. Graham was 'a natural' on a motorbike; a born mechanic; he taught me everything.

CHAPTER FIFTEEN

Learning - Newcastle High School

• 1 •

Using Rugby as a model, Newcastle High School was founded in 1874 and built in 1876 at a cost of £12,000 to cater for the better off who could afford the annual £25 tuition fee with an additional £50 for those who chose to board. It drew on the whole of the Potteries districts as well as taking a substantial number of boarders from a wider area.

Various Rugby men influenced its foundation and early years. Thereced was T H Green, the philosopher, who as Assistant Commissioner had recommended its establishment, F E Kitchener and Frederick Temple, the Bishop of Exeter and former head at Rugby who laid the foundation stone.

A Staffordshire Lad

The assembly hall was Big School, games were played in the Close and prefects were praeposters. Organised games included Fives, a forerunner of squash, played by hitting a hard ball with a thick, leather gloved hand against a multi-cornered wall. The Fives court was largely paid for by the first headmaster, F E Kitchener, who had been the assistant head at Rugby.

Academic standards were high. Pupils sat the London Matriculation examination and many went to university and the new 'redbrick' institutions. Of Kitchener's staff, two became professors of chemistry and nine headmasters. However, many of the leading families in the area tended to use the school as a preparatory establishment before sending their sons to public schools.

At the same time the Orme Girls' School was established on the opposite side of Stubbs Walks to respond to the increasing demand for female education.

At home, the 1949 summer holidays were a period of much excitement and activity. I received joining instructions and lists of requirements from the school. Navy blue cap with red rings, navy blue blazer with the school badge emblazoned on the top pocket, two red and black striped ties, white shirts, grey flannel trousers, grey socks, navy blue Burberry, leather satchel, black shoes, rugby boots and stockings, one white rugby shirt and one red and black hoops, (red and black were the West House colours to which I'd been allocated. The other house colours were green and black for East House, white and black for North House, and blue and black for School House). The list also included whites for cricket and vests, shorts and plimsolls for physical education. Getting kitted out involved many visits to Marsden's outfitters in Newcastle, the school's recommended provider, and the cost exceeded a staggering one hundred pounds.

• 2 •

The first day of term arrived and I set off for my new school, a distance of about two miles, with mixed feelings of self-consciousness, inner pride and some trepidation. I'd already planned the route that took me along Albany Road, through the Brampton playing fields and Station Walks, passed the railway station, along Water Street by the old police station to Marsh Street and Mount Pleasant. School started at 9.15 a.m., but new boys were asked to be there at 10.00 a.m. on the first day. We assembled in the Memorial Hall and then segregated into classes. Eleven plus pupils were streamed into the third year's A B and C, the third year being the first year of the senior school. The half dozen of us that had passed the thirteen plus were placed in Lower Four C, one year lower than our year group. This was to allow us to catch up on subjects such as Latin and French, which hadn't been taught to us hitherto.

The start and end of break times were signalled by a large bell that hung on an outer wall in the old quadrangle, and rung by the duty prefect. We had been warned that ragging new boys was a school tradition, so Graham Allman and I kept ourselves at a safe enough distance to observe all the fun, whilst at the same time giving ourselves scope to escape. The favourite practice was to de-bag the new boys, haul their trousers up the flagpole and watch the poor little souls shinning up to get them back.

The main entrance was from Mount Pleasant. To the left of the main door was Albert's den, the school porter, a jolly, bespectacled little man, fat with few teeth and beloved by all. The main corridor led to the memorial hall on the left and the Headmaster's study and home on the right. The Headmaster was Mr J M Todd, a quiet, thoughtful man who seemed to carry with him an expression of utter grief. His house was built at the western end of the main building, overlooking the upper and lower closes. He rarely failed to take morning assembly and his love of music was apparent. Morning assembly was a grand affair lasting for around twenty minutes. Prayers were shared and hymns sung from the black school hymnbook, a copy of which was given to every boy on the first day. Mr Todd often introduced us to new music. He would sing first in a quiet, plaintive sort of voice, and then we would practice until he was satisfied. One of these was 'We Vow to Thee Our Country' from Gustave Holst's Planet Suite, a piece of music that will forever transport me back to my old schooldays.

The school was well-equipped with science laboratories and lecture rooms, state of the art gymnasium, swimming pool, tennis and fives courts, every type of sports field, library, art studio with clay modelling facilities, kitchen and dining room. The memorial hall was huge with choir and organ at one end and a fully equipped stage at the other. The portraits of past head teachers lined the walls together with a list of those former pupils killed in the two world wars.

All staff wore their university gowns daily with the full regalia on prize days and special occasions. Prefects and house captains had special duties and responsibilities. Each class was allocated a prefect to carry out basic tasks such as attendance and minor supervision; ours was John Evason. House captains selected teams and organised inter-house competitions. Each House had its own House Master and meetings were convened regularly. West House meetings were held in the physics laboratory. Pupils were encouraged to keep abreast with current events and a wide selection of newspapers from the Times to the Daily Worker were delivered each day to the library. Number 19 Mount Pleasant was the school tuck shop. Each break time a stampede took place in order to be well placed to buy the goodies on offer, hot drinks, pastries and all things to whet the appetites of hungry boys.

Members of staff were specialists in their own right and mainly taught their own subjects. However, a teacher was allocated to each class. Mr Dudley taught French. He was one of the longest serving members of staff and had responsibility for boarders. Albert Miles was our sixth form tutor and mathematics teacher, Mr Boyd taught Latin, Mr Tams was our art teacher and physical education instructor assisted later by Len Williams formerly from the Orme Boys, Tommy Eyles, was a keep fit enthusiast and athletics' coach, Mr and Mrs Penrice both taught Geography and Mr Brocklehurst, a sallow complexioned, bespectacled, sadistic hard nut, taught History.

• 3 •

We quickly settled down in our new environment and started to make new friends. John Bate, Dad's cousin's son, Tuff (Graham) Bloor, my best pal, Peter Anderson, our doctor's son, Clive Dickin, son of a Chesterton draper, Peter Doorbar, a first class swimmer and artist, Roy Preston, a Gordon Pirie look-a-like who became an outstanding cross country runner, Graham Viggars and John Deeming, two Madeley lads, Eric Ward, son of a Silverdale miner, Brian Wright, who became my best friend on leaving school and John France, an expert in classical music. Also in our class were Tony Lee from the Chinese laundry in Newcastle, Gerald Martyn and Martin Ball, Keith Jones, Terry Underwood, Tony Brereton John Barber, and Gary Nicholson, whose parents lodged the half dozen or so boarders in their large house across from the school in

Lancaster Road. Sadly, Geoffrey Allman left school after the first year because his family moved to South Africa.

The first task was to create a weekly programme of classes, duration and location, the 'time-table'. This was the bible and was kept close by at all times. It was imperative that we turned up at the right classroom with the right text and exercise books, and completed homework at the right time. Punishment was dealt out liberally from lines and extra homework to beatings. The slipper, or pump, was administered regularly. We expected it and prepared for it. Peers were considered weak if they never had it, and popular if they had it regularly. In a masochistic way, some individuals deliberately offended to enhance their personal score.

It was a six-day week with four lessons on Saturday mornings, and sport on Wednesday and Saturday afternoons. Visits to see Stoke City were limited to school holidays, evening matches and Saturday afternoons when sport was cancelled, which was rare.

Having had two years of relatively high academic success, my confidence was somewhat dented by a distinct lack of comprehension in Latin and French. Latin was just a continual process of 'verb-learning', with no rhyme nor reason as to background and usefulness, only that *you will need it to get into university*. And it was true. Some highly intellectual sixth-form science students, who had failed Latin, couldn't get into higher education. However, French proved that I had no aptitude for languages. Mr Dudley, our French master, was one of the old school who taught his subject with enthusiasm and interest. He'd balance the language tuition with geographical and historical aspects, but no matter how much I enjoyed the latter, the former just would not stick.

The formidable Mr Brocklehurst taught history. He was a lean, rangy individual, slightly stooping, sallow complexioned, bespectacled with dark, hard staring eyes. He prowled around the classroom with his hands clasped behind his back like a hungry wolf, seeking to satisfy his insatiable appetite for beating unsuspecting young and ignorant heads with his knuckled hand, or sometimes rapping knuckles with the thin edge of a ruler, and regularly meting out large helpings of the pump with great energy and sadistic pleasure. And as if this wasn't enough to kill any enthusiasm I might have had for the subject, he bombarded us with dates and politics from the period 1821 to 1914. The industrial revolution, repealing the Corn Laws, the Pitts, Peel, Palmerston, Gladstone and Disraeli weren't subjects to set young minds alight. To his utter amazement I passed the History GCE ordinary level, but the success wasn't due to his tuition. I discovered that the examination included eight questions of which only four needed to be answered. For six months I pored over past papers and swatted up on the most often asked questions. Three of these were included in my exam' resulting in a pass.

On the contrary Geography was absorbing. This was a subject essential to my ultimate objective and I revelled in it. Books I'd read of Canada and South America had already whetted my appetite and I was thirsty for more. Our teacher was Mrs Penrice, the only female member of staff. Her husband also taught Geography, but only to senior school. Mrs Penrice was a quietly spoken, diminutive, almost dwarfish individual with a hooknose, protruding teeth and an old-fashioned rolled hairstyle. Quite often when she came into class she would say 'Open the windows; there's a smell of boy in here'.

Much of what I learnt in those days has stayed with me all of my life. Meteorology I found stimulating. She taught us to identify cloud formations such as cirrus and cirrus strata; the measurement of rainfall, atmospheric pressure and temperature using isobars and isotherms; cartography, the science of map-making and the National Grid; Mercator's projection; the social and economic effects, in fact she touched on almost every aspect associated with the geographical, geological, metrological, economic and social influences on the planet at that time and I passed my GCE examination with flying colours.

English has always come easy to me. I enjoyed writing and reading, but found Shakespeare particularly heavy going. We were taken to see the 'Hamlet' and 'Richard III' films with Lawrence Olivier, and the visual aspect helped to improve my understanding. The school had an annual reading competition that everyone entered. I never made it passed the first hurdle. It dawned on me later that my thick Potteries brogue was no contest with the articulation of the boys from the more well to do families. We were given 'Twelfth Night', Robert Louis Stevenson's 'Travels With a Donkey' and C S Forester's 'The Gun' for the English Literature GCE exam'. 'Twelfth Night' I learned parrot fashion. I devoted the rest of my concentration to 'Travels With a Donkey' and fortunately passed.

The interest in craft studies fired at the Orme was further stimulated at my new school and enhanced by a theoretical subject, technical drawing. This proved to be extremely valuable in later life and, to my delight, I passed the examination. Never having a natural ability in art, my progress was accelerated by the attention and enthusiasm of Mr Tams, so much so that after my second year I received a commendation at the annual prize giving. We were introduced to modelling in clay and associated processes such as glazing and firing. Peter Doorbar, who had a lot of talent, and myself were invited to attend interviews for model painters at Doulton's China factory, but I declined. I had other ideas for my future.

Religious Instructions and Mathematics simply bored me out of my mind and consequently resulted in total failure in the examinations. My previous success with Science turned into utter disaster. Although the Physics and Chemistry laboratories were well equipped, the unending theorems and laws did nothing to rekindle the spark, and it is with deep regret that I failed to sustain sufficient interest to generate the enthusiasm to succeed at even a lowly level. Although we were expected to learn, we were never taught how to learn, nor had the importance of education stressed enough upon us. A lack of motivation can turn to boredom and, in young minds, to mischief. As a consequence, many of us including myself, missed the bus.

• 4 •

My first love was sport and the facilities were second to none. Every pupil was allocated a locker in 'the dungeons'. The dungeons were sited in the basement below the Headmaster's study. They stank of unwashed bodies and sportswear. In the gym and on the sports' fields I was like a caged bird released. My skills at games were less than average, but were enhanced by my enthusiasm, fitness and competitiveness. During the first year we were introduced to Rugby Union. I discovered it to be a highly skilful and technical game that demanded not only strength and stamina, but also concentration, quick thinking and understanding. In all the years I played rugby at Newcastle I never fully understood its rules and intricacies. My lack of height was a problem, but it was compensated somewhat by my turn of speed and stamina. Turning out for the first game of the season was a pleasure I can recall even now; newly starched shirts and shorts, dubbined boots, bursting with energy, the smell of freshly mown turf, the buzz and the banter, that first blast on the whistle. And then after the game, the rush to the showers, the piles of muddy clothes and shoes, borrowing a comb, displaying war wounds, disputing points and arguing about the ownership of kit. We played in all sorts of conditions, the wetter and muddier the better. After a couple of years playing non-representative rugby, I was picked to play for my House and for the Colts, the school's junior team. I played at full back for the House and centre three quarter and hooker for the Colts. I was proud to represent the school, especially when we played our archenemy, Wolstanton Grammar. The visiting teams were provided with tea after the match, which at Wolstanton inevitably turned into a bun fight.

Cricket was my favourite game, but I wasn't good enough to play for the school. However, I was selected to play wicketkeeper for West House. Jimmy Hanley, my former friend, was captain, and our secret weapon was Eric Fletcher, an unbelievably fast bowler. During the season we spent our lunchtimes improving our batting and bowling skills in the nets on the Close, and our fielding on the cradle. The cradle was made of wooden laths fastened to a low trestle. The laths were spaced about one inch apart and bent into a coracle shape. The construction measured about six feet by four feet. The ball was hurled onto the cradle and flew off the corners of the laths in unpredictable directions at great speed, so sharpening the reflexes of the fielders. Everyone wore whites and sometimes as many as ten games took place on Wednesday and Saturday afternoons. The big events included games between the first team and the Old Boys and Keele University.

The only sport at which I represented the school at senior level was basketball. This was a new event for the school, introduced by our new PE teacher, Len Williams. Our star player was Selwyn Howle who'd been with me during my first year at the Orme. Selwyn's father had been killed in a car accident in Canada. He was a well known local entrepreneur in the coal industry. Selwyn, as the eldest of two sons took on the responsibility of the man of the house, and became serious minded beyond his years, but he was academically bright and a talented sportsman. After national service we both went to work for the English Electric Company at Stafford, and worked together on a number of projects. We became firm friends and used to support some of Stoke City's evening matches travelling straight from work to the ground. Selwyn left the Company in his late twenties to take up a job in Loughborough. Our careers brought us together yet again on a few occasions when I was the Chief Test Engineer and he was the visiting customer's inspector representing Hawker Siddeley.

Cross-country running was very popular and everyone ran, regardless of physical or medical handicaps. Initially, I had only a casual interest in the sport, but as I became more competitive and more aware of the need to keep fit, I threw myself into it wholeheartedly and, whilst still a junior, came fifteenth out of two hundred in the senior competition.

I became very interested in athletics, and in particular track and field events. Our athletics house captain was Kenny Slack. He gave me lots of encouragement and I spent many hours with him on the running track. My best achievement was runner-up in the junior school athletics championship, which included a win in the high jump and second in the hurdles. Many of our senior school athletes became county champions and it was a pleasure to see them perform.

It was rare for any school to have its own swimming pool and although I was banned from swimming because of my perforated eardrums, I was very proud of the facilities. The pool had diving boards, the deep end was nine feet and there were polo net facilities. I played a number of games of hockey and tennis. The former never attracted me too much, but the latter was to become my favourite teenage sport out of school.

I was at the forefront of anything that demanded a release of energy, and I enjoyed physical education equally as much as any sport. The gymnasium was well equipped with wall bars, ropes, rope ladders, beams, horse, box and buck. Len Williams was a hard taskmaster and took us through a range of gymnastics from simple to quite complicated. It was on one of these that I had my first serious accident. The legs of the horse were extended to their maximum. Many of the class had been eliminated at the lower levels and just a few of us were still competing. As I went into the final vault I pushed at the horse and, as I went over, it started to topple on top of me. I fell to the right and put out my right arm to save me. There was a very loud crack and I found the lower part of my arm at right angles to the upper part. Both the ulna and radius bones were severely fractured. I was told to lie on a mat until help arrived. The help was Mr Brocklehurst with that sadistic, superciolious grin on his face. He ordered four of the biggest boys to hold me down and then tried to pull the arm straight. When I almost passed out, he decided to dispatch me to the hospital. John Evason, the form prefect, who owned a car, took me. After an x-ray, I was taken to the plaster room where I was given anaesthetic. The arm was straightened and put into plaster. For the next eight weeks I became totally bored with my inactivity. Within the next nine months I also fractured each of my wrists, the left, during a fall whilst pole-vaulting and the right when I fell down the bank that separated the upper and lower closes when fielding on the boundary during a cricket match.

Football was not entertained at Newcastle High School, but during breaks 'Quad Soccer' was very popular. The three enclosed sides of the new quad' was perfectly designed for young, mad, keen football enthusiasts to kick a tennis ball about, and hell out of one another. There were no teams. Anyone wishing to play just joined in.

• 5 •

Indoors we played shove ha'penny and table cricket. All our hexagonal pencils were marked at one end with six ways of getting out, and at the other with the number of runs scored from one to six. We also played miniature cricket using a micro bat and a marble. In the sixth form we degenerated into pitch and toss and billiards played at the local Eighteen Tables, an establishment strictly out of bounds for all pupils!

During the second autumn term our class spent a week spud bashing at a farm near Loggerheads. Dad increased my normal intake of sandwiches from two rounds to eight. A bus took us to the farm and brought us home each day. We were placed in groups of five or six and spaced about fifty yards apart. As the farmer lifted a row of potatoes each group would stack them into piles. Battles between the different groups helped the days along. At the end of the week we were given five shillings, as many spuds as we could carry and a few pounds of damsons. During the following winter we were taken on a visit to the Rolls Royce factory at Derby.

A Staffordshire Lad

I was fascinated with the manufacturing processes of aero engines, but, like the spud bashing, I remember mostly the feeling of release from school, playing records on Granddad Sam's old portable wind-up gramophone on the bus and the laughs we had.

The 1952 election created a great deal of national interest and the school decided to hold its own mock election. It was a time that trusted friends became antagonists. Never before was I made so aware of my humble background. The right wing attitudes of the 'well off' boys screwed the socialist minority into the ground.

Also in 1952 two tragic events stunned the school. On the sixth of February we were told of the death of King George VI. Everyone was speechless. The death of this quietly spoken man, so unwilling to become king following the abdication of his elder brother Edward, put the entire school in a state of shock. This was the man with whom we had shared our Christmas afternoons, crowded round our wireless sets to listen to his Christmas messages presented in his shy, lisping voice. This was the man who refused to move his family from London during the blitz and this was the man so loved that the entire nation was plunged into mourning - everyone was saddened at his passing. The funeral took place on Friday 15 February and as a show of respect, Parliament put off its contentious business, theatres and cinemas closed, churches were packed and after the two minutes silence had been observed, factory and fire brigade sirens were sounded, traffic stopped and people stood in the streets with their heads bowed.

The second incident took place later on a beautiful summer's day. We were stretched out on the grass during lunch break when I heard the familiar sound of a Meteor Mark 2 fighter. To our delight it circled directly above us and then started to perform an amazing series of aerobatics, but our delight quickly turned to dismay, when, coming out of a loop, there was a loud bang and, to our horror, the plane crashed just north of the school. We discovered later that the pilot was an old boy who had recently completed his training. He had apparently steered the plane onto Porthill cricket ground in order to miss the populated area and narrowly missing St. Margaret's School.

Our year, in 1953, was only the second to take the General Certificate of Education (GCE). The School and Higher School Certificates were replaced with the GCE on 26 April 1948. The difference was that a minimum of five subjects had to be passed to achieve a School Certificate. With the GCE each individual subject could be awarded a pass. Having passed only four subjects, the right and proper thing to have done would have been to leave school, get a job and pay back some of the money Mum and Dad had invested in me. Already seventeen, and with my eyes firmly set on joining the RAF the following year, I stayed at school and became a sixth former. Albert Miles was our form master who tried his best to convert me to a maths buff without success. Our classroom was the chemistry lecture room, traditionally tiered so that we looked down on dear Albert's bald spot.

My final year was enjoyable, marred by one unfortunate incident. It was the morning break. We were having our bottles of milk and our snacks. As usual screwed up lunch paper and apple cores were flying around the room. An apple core hit me and I redirected it at Michael Colclough, the form captain, who was playing shove ha'penny on Albert's desk. The apple core buried itself in Michael's ear. He was, understandably, not amused. In fact he was so mad he stormed up to me and started a fight. I swung back in retaliation and unfortunately cut his eyelid badly. The blood was streaming down his face and I had to put an end to it. Fighting was just not tolerated at the school and sixth formers were supposed to set an example. I knew that action would be taken and the next day Albert asked the guilty party to own up. On the way to the Headmaster's study he whispered that I must pack a hefty wallop as Michael's eye had needed six stitches. Mr Todd was very distressed and debated whether or not to expel me. In the end he selected one of his many canes and gave me six severe lashes on the hindquarters, very light punishment indeed.

As sixth formers we were able to go to the school dances. These were opportunities to show off our latest girls and prove to mates that there was more in the wardrobe than a school uniform. Other schools held dances too and, if we were lucky, we'd get invited to them. I joined the CEWC society. I think it stood for Christian Education and World Citizenship, but it was really a debating society and another means to meet different people of our own age.

As June 1954 approached, I became increasingly excited at the prospect of leaving school. The time was nearing for me to move out of boyhood idleness. At the Headmaster's suggestion, we circulated our hymnbooks for friends to insert autographs on their favourite hymns. My national service papers had been sent, completed and returned, and Tuff Bloor's dad, who was a director at Spode's pottery firm, had arranged a temporary job for me in the interim.

• 6 •

I was now fully developed, five feet ten inches, eleven stones and three pounds, extremely dress conscious and raring to go. My last day at school came and went without a second thought for what Newcastle High School had given to me. As I went out of the Mount Pleasant gate for the last time my mind was full of what was before me, but so many times throughout my life I have wished that I could have said thank you to someone. Education like life is taken for granted. My parents gave me the gift of life. Education is a gift for life. It prepares us for the future, encourages us to work together meaningfully and helps us to realise our potential. We tend to overlook the professionalism and dedication of teachers, the hard work it takes to achieve qualifications, experience and skills in order to pass on knowledge to their pupils, aware that their only reward is a job well done. So it was with a great deal of pleasure and some trepidation that I found myself re-visiting my old school again almost forty two years to the day that I'd left it.

Fortunately, my career had involved me with the education and development of young people and I had responsibility for assisting local education through business and enterprise. As a result, I was able to visit the school professionally in order to offer this help, and also to say hello to a few ghosts. As a consequence, on 19 June 1996, I turned into The Avenue, the last, painful leg of so many cross-country runs, only this time in the comfort of my company car. Left into Lancaster Road with the main edifice of the school across The Close, then left again into Mount Pleasant passing the old tuck shop, now a private home. The main entrance was locked as a precaution following the Dunblaine massacre, a sign of the times, so I parked in the headmaster's car park.

I was shown into the secretary's office, originally part of the headmaster's home. We chatted for a while and she explained some of the changes that had taken place over the last fourteen years. Newcastle-under-Lyme School is now an Independent Day School for boys and girls formed in 1981 through the amalgamation of Newcastle High and the

Orme Girl's Schools. As I sat there, that same old feeling of foreboding and trepidation came over me. I crossed my legs involuntarily to stop my knees knocking. I was invited into the office of the Principal, Dr R M Reynolds. He went through the usual formalities of welcome before doing the tour. We started in the old part of the school. Upstairs the old kitchen and dining room had been converted into classrooms; downstairs had changed very little with the main corridor and classrooms much as I remembered them. The main entrance had an interesting display of school caps demonstrating how they had changed throughout the history of the school. I noticed that the type I'd worn was third from the last – the familiar red and black rings looking particularly dated with its large beck. It seems school caps became obsolete during the 1960's. On the opposite wall were the winners' names of various sporting trophies. I couldn't remember seeing them before. I pointed out old Albert's office, the popular school porter. Dr Reynolds was quite interested; no one seemed to know what purpose it had previously served. The chemistry lecture room, my last classroom, and science laboratories had been converted into the new kitchen and dining room. The old gymnasium had become the library and computer room. A new gym had been built adjacent to the quadrangle, now totally enclosed.

We strolled across The Close discussing the changes and ethos of the school. We carried on to the swimming pool and old fives court before returning to the school buildings. Finally I was taken into the memorial hall with its gallery and partially restored organ. On the walls were pictures of former headmasters amongst them J M Todd smiling down at me as if to say 'Didn't I give you a damn good licking?' Or, as I prefer to think, 'So glad you called in to say thank you at last'. And I did, and I do thank all of my schools for trying with the greatest of difficulty to make something of their oft times reluctant pupil.

I'm ashamed to admit that I didn't make the most of my education. I was too easily distracted by non-academic pursuits. I was a daydreamer. It's true that I was not inclined towards the sciences and I was deeply affected and disappointed to discover that maths and science were mandatory requirements for flying crew. I had decided to join the Royal Air Force in spite of this disappointment, and to be associated with aircraft in any respect was some compensation.

As a result of my visit I was able to donate, and provide the training for, a comprehensive package of computer aided design software specifically formulated for education purposes; just a small 'thank you' for an excellent, broad-based education received with much gratitude, and, of course, it went some small way towards satisfying my conscience for not making the most of it.

CHAPTER SIXTEEN

FLITTING

• 1 •

On 10 March 1953 our sheltered feeling of family completeness was shattered by the death of Grandma Titley. She finally lost her battle with cancer from which she had suffered for more than five years. She had never cultivated any affection in me. I can't remember a single occasion when she showed me one iota of interest, but I felt her loss. As a family, it seemed to me, we had always been involved with her. Dad, as the only child, was the epitome of the loyal and devoted son, never missing a week without visiting his parents. Just before Grandma died, we gathered round her bed to say our farewells. Dad asked each of us to kiss her goodbye, but I refused. There was just nothing there for me. However, her funeral made a deep impression on me. It was the first I'd been to, and it was the first time I'd seen my dad and granddad cry. I cried myself as I followed my granddad through the graveyard to Grandma's final resting place. It brought home to me the fragility of life and the finality of death, the realisation that life wasn't all good times and that everything has its end.

Her death brought a dramatic change to all of our lives. Granddad had worn himself out looking after his Molly. He'd worshipped the ground she walked on. His entire world was shattered. His home had no bathroom, only gas lighting and no modern comforts. He was completely undomesticated and unable to provide even the basic necessities for himself. The difficult decision was what to do with him. There was no room for him in our home, but it was clear that he couldn't be left to fend for himself.

Around the same time, Mr Lockett, our landlord, had intimated that he wanted to sell our house and gave Dad first offer. We lived hand-to-mouth and hadn't a penny of savings to our name. Granddad agreed to take up a £700 pounds' mortgage on his house to pay the sitting tenant's cost of ours to Mr. Lockett. Dad and I then spent a feverish two months getting the house into a saleable condition. It was advertised and eventually sold for £1,450; a profit of more than a hundred per cent. Dad was able to pay back the mortgage and had cash in hand to modernise Granddad's house. 57 Diglake Street was to become our new home.

I loved my home. I was used to it, and to the area. I had lots of good friends. It's true that as I developed, new friendships were made. Although Graham and me went to different schools, and our association became a little stretched, we still found time for each other. I knew I was going to miss him and I did. I still do.

When we first heard that we were going to flit, both my mother and I were devastated. Joan and Mary weren't that bothered. Joan was now engaged to Ken Martyn, an R.A.F. colleague of her former fiancé Denis Rushton. They were

A Staffordshire Lad

planning to get married within the next twelve months, and Mary had her own life planned out. Mum had never liked Bignall-End since a bad experience during the early years of her marriage. I still find it difficult to express my true feelings when I learnt that we were going to leave our home; only those who have experienced it will understand. It was like having the roots torn out of my life and, although only five miles away, transplanted into some foreign soil. It was by no means a grand house, quite the reverse. It was poorly built and in a deprived area, but it was home, the place where I'd been born, the only home I'd ever known. I had never thought of it with any kind of warmth until I learned that I was going to leave it. The protection, shelter and sheer homeliness of the place were to be taken from me, and not even the hard shell of youth could protect me from feeling so bereft. Between those four walls I had learnt to walk and talk, had slept and played, became ill and got well, had laughed and cried, and had been happy and sad. It was the place that had helped to shape me. And it was with a feeling of deep sadness and sentiment, a new experience for me, that I wandered around the rooms of our home with Mum, with lumps in our throats and tears in our eyes, for the last time to say goodbye and thank you. Once again for the last time we stared through that same bedroom window together. I left Mum there to say goodbye to that most personal of her rooms, while I went into mine; the tiny box room where I'd weaved all my dreams, held midnight chats with Graham across our dark gardens, sheltered my most precious possessions and guarded my innermost secrets. I looked across to the backs of the houses in Orton Road - the block - where all the wars had been fought, all the battle wounds suffered and all the friendships made.

A Staffordshire Lad

> *Round the next corner and in the next Street*
> *Adventure lies in wait for you.*
> *Oh, who can tell what you may meet*
> *Round the next corner and in the next Street!*
> *Could life be anything but sweet*
> *When all is hazardous and new?*
> *Round the next corner and in the next Street*
> *Adventure lies in wait for you.*

EFA Geach (Oxford)

It was quiet, almost as though everyone had moved indoors to mourn our leaving. We shed our tears as we looked at the small corner in the bathroom where we'd all cowered together when the air raid sirens sounded. We looked at the marks on the lino' where our pieces of austere furniture had sat, and at the now cold fireplace where we'd all sat so many times in a tight family circle, now freshly blacked for its new owners; only we knew the hardships of keeping the fires burning in it. The furniture van already loaded and waiting, we gave the old place a final glance, said our silent farewells and closed the gate on our life there. We climbed into the cab and, with heavy hearts, set off to a place where both of us least wanted to be.

• 2 •

Dad worked very hard to turn 57 Diglake Street into a comfortable place for us to live, but it never became a home to me. For me, our flitting signalled the end of family life in its entirety, as we had known it, forever. Joan and Mary slept in the box room and I had to share Granddad's room. I hated every moment of it.

A Staffordshire Lad

The money Dad had made through the sale of the house was spent on the installation of electricity and a new bathroom, flush toilet and garage. There was also enough for a new washing machine, vacuum cleaner, cooker and a car. Mum and Dad had never had it so good. Dad had brokered a good deal and these extra luxuries compensated somewhat for the disappointment of moving.

Ironically, I was the first to settle down, helped considerably by the fact that many of my friends from school lived in the area. Brian Wright, who was in my class, became my best friend, John 'Rags' Riley, Phil Harrison, both from Boon Hill, Ken Keeling, son of the landlord of 'The Butcher's Arms' at Audley and Ken Tarrant and Selwyn Booth, all from school, took me into their circle of friends that included Derek Rowley and Malcolm Eardley who went to Wolstanton Grammar, Marcia Rowley, Derek's sister who was Brian's girlfriend, Wendy Daniels, Gwyneth Pierpoint and Keith Chesters. I had never been blessed with so many good friends of my own age. The following fifteen months proved to be a happy-go-lucky period in my teenage years. I was introduced to the socials at the chapel hall in the Old Road, skiffle, jazz, Jack Jackson's 'Top Twenty' from Radio Luxemburg, Nat King Cole, Frank Sinatra, Johnny Ray, Frankie Lane, Chris Barber, Johnnie Dankworth and Cleo Lane, Humphrey Littleton and Ottilie Patterson, Lonnie Donegan and Johnny Duncan and the Blue Grass Boys.

We gathered mainly at the Bignall-End Cricket Club at the top of Boon Hill where we played billiards and table tennis and planned future outings. These included visits to the theatre to see our favourite musicians and occasionally to the pictures. On Good Fridays everyone made their way to Jacob's Ladder for a picnic and a day out, and over Christmas, the inevitable parties. Now and again we'd go to the evening service at Audley church, or walk the local lanes and fields.

I was fanatical regarding sport and played tennis most summer evenings on the courts opposite the chapel in Old Road. It was here that I met Clive Rhodes and Gerald Maddox from Audley, but my favourite opponent was Gwyneth Pierpoint. She lived adjacent to the courts on New Road. Her parents owned the furniture shop there – the green wooden place – as it was known. She was fiercely competitive and a strong player. Sometimes, during the school holidays, we'd play all day, and she gave as good as she took. Ken Tarrant, her boyfriend at the time, was also a strong player.

In spite of the fun, leaving Cross Heath left an enormous hole. Life was never the same. The change brought a feeling of unsettlement and a need to readjust. I missed my former life and friends and, most of all, my old home.

CHAPTER SEVENTEEN

FLYING

• 1 •

Briefing over, flight plan agreed, I followed the pilot across the grass apron at the very rural Sleap aerodrome in Shropshire to the sturdy little strut-braced, high winged Cessna 140. The tiny cockpit had side-by-side seating for two and dual controls and instrumentation. We strapped ourselves in and fitted the earphones and microphones. Communication could be switched to internal or local air traffic control. The pilot fired the Continental C-90-12 ninety horse power engine, checked the controls and taxied to the far end of the runway facing into the breeze, the wind sock barely lifting. It was one of those glorious, mid-summer days that seem only to occur in England, and then, all too infrequently. The countryside, freshly greened by the recent rain, was battling hard with the increasing heat to hang on to small pockets of mist. The sun, at its zenith, was set in a clear blue sky with just a few wisps of cirrus over the Welsh hills. 'Beware the Hun in the sun'. How many times had I read that?

Cleared for take off, revolutions increased to maximum, brakes released, we were airborne before I had time to draw breath. We circled the small aerodrome set a north-easterly course and climbed steadily to our prescribed ceiling of seven thousand feet before throttling down to a cruising speed of around ninety miles an hour.

As we crossed the Shropshire/Staffordshire border, just north of Market Drayton, control of the aircraft was passed to me. I was in my element. The controls were extremely sensitive and it took me a little time to put the plane on an even keel. The Cessna has a range of just less than four hundred nautical miles and our estimated round trip of ninety miles left a good deal in reserve, that is, as long as the tanks were fully filled before we started out – it did cross my mind! Over Trentham Gardens we changed to an easterly course and followed the route of the new A51 from Hanford to Meir – a ribbon of red clay littered with large earth removers and lorries. Just over the new Meir Park development, we headed south and followed the Levels. I picked out Hilderstone church and then my own home which we circled a few times before heading back to Sleap. As we came into land, the runway rushed up to us at an alarming speed. We touched down gently and immediately lifted off again just for the hell of it, did a circuit and came down finally, just one hour after taking off.

I was sixty and the flight was a birthday gift from my wife, Ann. It was the first time I had ever piloted a plane, and it was worth waiting for.

• 2 •

I have been interested in aeroplanes for all of my life. During the Second World War I was weaned on the roar of the

Rolls Royce Merlin engines that powered the illustrious Spitfires, the throbbing of bombed-up Wellingtons, Hamdens, Halifaxs and Lancasters as they made their way eastwards, and the sinister, intermittent hum of German bombers during their nightly raids. The model of the Lancaster bomber carved out of wood so patiently by Uncle Albert Dale while recuperating from a brain tumour operation and given to me when I was four, helped fire my imagination.

From those early years to the present day I can't hear a plane without searching the skies for it. 'Biggles' was my first hero and I started to read the books shortly after joining Newcastle library when I was ten and became totally immersed in every one. The excitement so sharpened my senses that I could hear the throb of the radial engines and smell the 'dope' emanating from the pages. I read them all, more than once. The characters became my dearest friends. I just had to be a pilot.

From paper aeroplanes to kites to gliders to model aeroplanes was a natural progression. Petrol engine powered model-planes had barely been introduced and the cost was prohibitive. Radio control was a dream in the comics. The only control was by a hand-held device with wires attached to the plane and these were complicated and out of the range of my pocket. However, there were lots of reasonably priced elastic-powered models on offer and it was on these that I cut my teeth. The elastic band was attached between the tailplane and the propeller and energised by winding the prop' to its maximum before releasing. Frog produced a number of models. Working with Graham, we built a number of gliders of various size and design and flew them in the four fields, usually by the railway as the large slope to the brook gave a natural uplift.

A Staffordshire Lad

When I was eleven, Mr Heywood our next door but one neighbour, gave me an almost completed model aircraft with a wingspan of three feet, covered in white silk and strengthened by 'dope'. This was a real feather in my cap because Mr Heywood had considered all the boys in the neighbourhood before deciding to give it to me. I kept it under my bed only pulling it out occasionally to work on and, one day, I was devastated to find that Mary had smashed the mainplane and fuselage to match wood. I never discovered how or why she had done it.

Graham and I occasionally cycled over to Tern Hill Aerodrome near Market Drayton, a round trip of more than thirty miles. Lying on the perimeter grass, we'd watch the planes landing and taking off. We saw our first jet aircraft there, the twin boom Vampire fighter, and also a Lancaster bomber demonstrating its fantastic versatility and ability to fly on one of its four engines. It was whilst watching the aircraft at Tern Hill that I became interested in aeronautical and airfield design. I noticed that when the planes touched down, the static tyres caused a great deal of friction as they hit the tarmac, demonstrated by a puff of smoke caused by burning rubber. I spent ours designing wheels that had fins pressed into the wheel casting so that when the undercarriage was lowered, the air stream caused the wheels to rotate and so reduce the wear on the tyres. I also designed convex and concave runways to provide more lift when taking off, and more deceleration when landing. I discovered later that this type of design had been used on aircraft carriers and is still in service today. I learned that my teacher, Mrs Gassick, at the Orme Boys, had been a good friend of R J Mitchell the famous local designer of the Spitfire. He was born in Talke and was a maths wizard with an intuitive grasp of aerodynamics. Mitchell designed the Spitfire in 1935 and sadly died in

1937, aged 47, never to see the plane's triumph during the Second World War. Mrs Gassick used to relate stories and experiences of this extraordinary man, each one fuelling my interest and my ambition to become a flyer.

At thirteen I joined the Air Training Corps and one of my proudest moments was the evening I came home completely kitted out in the blue uniform and forest cap. I was taught the rudiments of drill, the Morse code, aircraft recognition and shooting with a 2.2 mms rifle on the barracks' range.

Throughout my teens I had only one ambition, to join the Royal Air Force and become a pilot. How big was my disappointment then, when I discovered that not only was I not going to be a pilot, but that the nearest I was going to get to flying was in a service plane on my way home on leave?

CHAPTER EIGHTEEN

SERVING

• 1 •

National Service was, perhaps, one of the biggest impacts to hit young men between 1947 and 1960. More than two million boys born before and during the Second World War were conscripted into the three services.

Contrary to common belief, National Service had a very short life. From the passing of the National Service Act in 1947 to the decision to end conscription, covered a span of only ten years. Both politically and militarily, it was viewed as a temporary expedient, a necessary evil.

At the outbreak of the Second World War, and for the second time in the twentieth century, the armed services were forced to absorb a generation of civilians. In May 1937 the Military Training Act required all men of twenty years of age to undergo six months training in the armed services. At the outbreak of war this was superseded by the National Service (Armed Forces) Act that required all males from eighteen to forty one years of age to do military service for the duration

A Staffordshire Lad

of the emergency. This resulted in many conscripts having to serve for two or more years after the war in order to retain the necessary skills.

In 1947 the National Service Act was passed. The issue had been a political football for some time both within parties and across benches, and at the same time getting poked and prodded by the Chiefs of Staff of all three services. National Service of one year, eighteen months and two years were all considered, and, because of the expensive and extended training needs for skilled craftsmen and technicians, a two-year term was finally agreed. Influenced by the rise of Russia as an atomic power, the Berlin Airlift, the Korean War and the loss of India, the debate on military recruitment continued to rumble on.

In 1957 the newly elected Conservative government, seeking to create an image as a cost-cutting party, declared their intention to end National Service and deemed that there would be no call-up later than 1960 resulting in the last national servicemen leaving in 1962.

At a time when the country was attempting to pay back its debts incurred by the war, and to re-generate the economy, national service also had a negative impact. It caused disruption to higher education, skills training and employment. Deferment arrangements helped to ease the problems, but employers had to keep jobs open until their employees returned. The disruption caused to young men is not to be underrated. Fear of the unknown, the strain on relationships of those who were married, the indecision in identifying careers, the lack of continuity and the disorientation after demobilisation were all issues of concern. Like me, many conscripts were persuaded to sign on as three-year regulars with the incentive of more pay. The main reason was to provide a major source of so-called regular recruits. What wasn't explained adequately was the requirement to fulfil a period of up to six years reserve following demobilisation.

• 2 •

Monday 22 November 1954, Mary's twenty first birthday, eventually arrived and I said my goodbyes to an emotional Mum, Dad and Mary before they left for work, packed up my few essentials as indicated on the R.A.F. checklist, shook Granddad's hand and was off up the street to the bus stop at the Pump as excited and as light-hearted as a five-year-old. As the bus pulled away, Dad came out of Swettenhams shop at the top of Diglake Street, where he was temporarily working, to see me off. His capacious, round, dependable and familiar shape filled the doorway. He was wearing his spotless white overall and long apron and he had tears in his big, honest blue eyes as he waved me out of sight; an image that's filed away in my memory bank for the rest of my conscious life. And an image that caused me to reflect on my past young life, the good parents I had and the struggles they'd had to raise their three children to adulthood. Joan had left five months earlier, after her wedding, to live in Cambridge and, ultimately to the far corners of the world, rarely to see her roots again. Mary was to be married in just three months time and now, here was I, off to who knows where; all three of us to fledge in less than a year.

I arrived at Stoke Station at 9.15 a.m. This was my first experience of travelling by train on my own and I was excited at the prospect. For the first time I was conscious of the activity and surprised at the hustle and bustle of the place. Everything and everywhere evoked a sense of movement. I was more than aware that change was afoot and new horizons beckoning. The waiting trains were snorting steam and belching smoke as if, like me, bursting with impatience to be on their way, like rampant racehorses at the starting gate. Advertisements designed to encourage travellers to change destinations and visit unheard of places, if not now then at some later, more convenient date; the rattle of sack, and iron-wheeled flat trucks as they were pushed and pulled up and down the rough platforms; doors slamming to admit passengers relieved at last to be on the right train and followed by porters in greasy black uniforms and caps waiting patiently for tips after securing the luggage in the net racks above the seats; doors re-opening to allow passengers to buy last minute items such as newspapers and magazines from the W. H. Smith's stall, or a bar of chocolate from the cast iron Nestle and Cadbury slot machines; the shrill whistles and green flags as the guards at last got the trains away; the slamming shut of the last few open doors by the guard; the lowering and the raising of windows with the leather straps as goodbyes were made, all added to the thrill of the day.

I spotted another boy with a wide-eyed expectant "What's going to happen to me?" look on his face, and holding the familiar R.A.F. travel warrant. It was good to have someone with which to share the journey and exchange a bit of conversation. We arrived at Wolverhampton and found our way to the R.A.F. recruiting office where we were joined with about fifteen other new recruits. A jolly sergeant welcomed us into the service using our first names from his list, the first and last time they would be used for the duration by any NCO or officer. It was here that I made my first mistake, something I've since regretted. I should have corrected him when he called me 'Bill' instead of 'Harry', but the truth is I hadn't the courage, so the name stuck throughout my service, and beyond, which is another story. At Wolverhampton we were given new travel warrants to Bedford and transported back to the station. At Bedford we were collected and taken to Cardington, the R.A.F.'s base for the receiving and kitting out of new recruits.

R.A.F. Cardington was famous for its association with the R100 and R101 airships. The massive hangar and the stanchions to which they were anchored were still in place. Sir Barnes Wallis, the famous designer of the Wellington bomber and the bouncing bomb, had worked here, as had Nevil Shute, the famous author whose books I was to read and re-read many times. It was also the parachute training camp with its jumping platforms and soft landing facilities, and for training barrage balloon operators. Later it was used for the restoration of historic aircraft and storage. There was much to see and much to do at Cardington.

On arrival we were introduced to the infamous barrack blocks and allocated bed spaces, and to the equally infamous 'airmen's mess'. The first day included a visit to the barber's. "How would you like it sir?" Incredible, after all those horror stories! "Well, leave the quiff; not too much off the top and taper the neck," I replied. Five minutes later we were examining each other's *style,* a regimental short back and sides!

Then there was the medical. Sadistic orderlies administered jabs like hot-blooded picadors. We were then ordered to strip and stand on a table like carcasses hanging in a butcher's shop whilst the Medical Officer suspended our private parts on the end of a pencil like parrots on a perch, so that he could carry out what was called an F.F.I. (Free From Infection). The rest of the week we were subjected to a plethora of baffling detail including the distribution of every item of clothing 'for the use of'; dress uniform and working blue; towels; pyjamas; gloves; drawers cellular white; vests cellular white; braces; denims; mug and irons; mess tin; gym kit and plimsolls; the inevitable mug shots for our identity cards, the notorious form 1250 together with threats of death should we lose it; the 'housewife', a white cotton wallet that contained everything to sew on buttons and darn socks; a brass button stick to slide behind brass buttons and cap badges to stop the Brasso contaminating the uniform; the famous white kit bag with the air force blue ring around the middle, and name and service number stamped in black; the laughs when someone was issued with something that didn't fit; the anguish when it happened to you; the Queen's shilling; the fear of the unknown; the fun, the tears and the foundation of comradeship; the Saturday night camp dance that helped relieve some of the tensions.

I had become an erk; an AC Plonk; 3519900 Aircraftsman second class Titley. My service number as indelibly printed into my memory as it had been onto my 1250 and the cotton tapes that had been sewn into my clothes, and branded into my soul as deep as into my knife fork and spoon. I'd become a number, a statistic, and an article 'for the use of'. Such was life at Cardington and there the fun and laughter ended for some considerable time. Towards the end of the week we visited the tailors for final adjustments to our uniforms, and then we had to pack up our civilian clothes in brown paper ready for posting to our homes. It was four weeks and another life later when I was able to feel the comfort and freedom of wearing my own clothes once more.

• 3 •

Just one week after leaving home we were on the move again. We had been separated into groups for transport to one of the notorious square-bashing camps. The Schools of Recruit Training were Number Three Padgate; Number Four Wimslow; Number Five West Kirby; Number Seven

Bridgnorth; Number Ten Melksham and Number Eleven Hednesford. The Snowdrops, as we called the R.A.F. Police on account of their white peaked caps, herded us into our respective groups at Bedford station; our kit bags were loaded into the goods van. The journey seemed unending. Some played cards; some just stared out of the windows. Others read newspapers and the more mischievous set the papers on fire for the sheer hell of it. On the run-in to Crewe station I saw the familiar spots at Madeley, and guessed Granddad Sam would be stoking up the fire to finish cooking his rice pudding in the oven; then the Josiah Wedgwood monument on Talke Hill and knew that just below there Granddad Arthur would be preparing the 'pillings' for his chickens and Dad would be slicing the bacon and running the shop in his quiet, efficient way.

We stopped at Crewe station and were given packs of stale sandwiches and mugs of stewed tea. Our next and final stop was Lime Street station at Liverpool. The first thing that greeted us was a loud, abusive Scottish voice belonging to the infamous Corporal Hawkins. He yelled out the name and last three numbers on each of the kit bags with an urgent "On the double you 'orrible little man!" Surely we were not destined to spend the next eight weeks with such as he? Wrong! he was to be our N.C.O. in charge; our drill instructor; a very sharp thorn in our sides for the duration of the depersonalisation and indoctrination process. What sheer bad luck, but the die was cast.

We were told en route that our destination was West Kirby although no one seemed to know where it was. Somewhere near Liverpool we'd heard. West Kirby is situated at the most westerly tip of the Wirral peninsular that separates the estuaries of the Dee and the Mersey in the borough of Hoylake. To get there we were packed into R.A.F. lorries for

A Staffordshire Lad

the last leg of the journey. On arrival we were allocated to three wooden barracks, thirty to each. Mine was No. 433 and I was fortunate to have with me four of the lads that I'd teamed up with at Cardington, Tony Rees from Exeter, Jim Rowley from Plymouth, a married man, Jock Pugh from Aberdeen and John Ryan, a ballet dancer from Kings Lynn. After dropping our kit bags by our beds, we were double-quick marched to the mess complete with mug and irons. The food was basic, but it filled the gaps in our stomachs. The tea was strong and stewed, rumoured to be laced with 'bromide' to suppress carnal desire. Outside the mess a tank of boiling water provided the means of washing and sterilising mugs and irons. We quickly learned to hold them by their tips to avoid scalding hands and fingers, or losing them forever in the depths of the murky tank.

Back at the billet, Corporal Hawkins was waiting to pour out his worst. We were each issued with two sheets, five blankets, one pillow and a pillowslip. He demonstrated how beds must be made and how bedding must be folded each morning. The blankets and sheets must be individually folded and placed wafer fashion, blanket-sheet-blanket-sheet-blanket with a blanket folded around the whole and with the pillow on the top making a neat, square-angled stack. The remaining blanket was used to cover the palliasse. We were also allocated rotational duties which included cleaning latrines; stove cleaning, coke stacking, fire lighting and general cleaning; floor cleaning – the brown lino had to be maintained to a mirror-like finish. Ronuk was first pasted onto the floor then a bumper was used to bring up the shine. The bumper had a hinged, heavy, padded weight attached to the stale and was slid in both directions with great energy to achieve a satisfactory result. A pile of neatly stacked felt pads was provided at the hut entrance for placing under feet and sliding to one's bed space.

We were each issued with a 303 rifle, a pull-through and a piece of cotton waste called 'four by two', on account of its size, for cleaning the barrel. The rifles were stored in a rack at the end of the billet. We were each issued with a laundry card allowing us to have a maximum of twelve items washed weekly, although it wasn't uncommon to see a clutter of clothing draped around the stove at night. The stove was the central point for discussion. We gathered round it to air our differences, share our confidences and get to know each other whilst at the same time carry on with the eternal bull.

We were informed that 'lights out' was at 2200 hours sharp, and that we would be woken at 0615 hours. Working blue uniforms were to be pressed, buttons cleaned, boots polished and we were to be standing by our beds for inspection at 0730 sharp. Many of us dazed, distressed and demoralised stood in groups discussing all issues past week, present and immediate future, some in tears and others already buckling down to prepare for the morning. Although somewhat disappointed at the misfortune of having been placed under possibly the most sadistic N.C.O in the service, I had mentally prepared myself for the worst and considered each issue as a challenge to be overcome. I had been, sometimes unconsciously, conditioning myself for a life of discipline for the last few years. I'd heard all the horror stories and considered how I should react if placed in difficult situations.

The following morning, in a state of bleary-eyed semi-consciousness, we raced each other to the latrines. The insufficient number of washbasins meant that those who didn't make it first had less time to prepare for inspection and, at worst, miss breakfast. No plugs for the basins; just screwed up pieces of toilet paper. Plugs were a valuable asset and, if you owned one, it meant carrying it around with you. Also there were insufficient loos and toilet paper. Queuing was the norm and all sorts of ideas, suggestions and derisive remarks were generated to hurry along those in the act. We longed for the return of the First World War communal toilet that consisted of a long plank with holes conveniently placed for sitting on, privacy panels and a continually running drain situated below to carry everything. To speed things along, a screwed up newspaper was set on fire and floated down the drain. If only!

"Stand by your beds!" followed by a few derogatory expletives. "Attention! officer present!" These were the words that greeted us every morning at 7.30 a. m. Most days we were up at 5.30 preparing for the early morning inspections. No foot pads for officers and N.C.O's. Their studs and steel tips ripped into the highly polished lino. All windows wide open in spite of the cold December weather; bedding checked for correct folding with rule and set square; substandard stacks hurled through the offenders' windows; bed spaces, cupboards, latrines all inspected with absolute thoroughness. The slightest imperfection brought the Hawkins' wrath down heavily on the guilty party. Each week there was a full kit layout. Each item had a specific place on the bed and Hawkins knew it to the last tiny detail. Breakfast was at 0700 hours. A piece of toad-in- the-hole and a mug of stewed tea was normally all we had.

The early weeks were devoted to continuous square bashing in all weathers until we eventually marched and drilled in unison. This was interspersed with physical training, assault course training, shooting practice using 303 rifles and Bren guns. The Bren gun was an air-cooled gas-operated submachine gun that was first used in the Second World War. It required a team of two to operate it, a gunner and a gunner's mate whose job was to change magazines and release trapped gases that caused misfiring. Although a less than accurate marksman with the 303, I became quite useful with the Bren. The skill of using the Bren was not only in its firing, but also in the process of dismantling and assembly. There was serious competition to be the first blindfolded pair to have the gun fully assembled.

Bayonet practice had quite an affect on most of us. It wasn't the practice as much as the realisation that a foot or so of cold steel had to be thrust and twisted into the gut of another human being. Although 'the enemy' were bags of straw suspended on a gantry, the exercise was quite nauseating.

We were issued with service respirators and exposed to mustard gas in the gas chamber. We were subjected to the boring indoctrination films and lectures and taught the rudiments of map reading and living off the land. The latter was called reliability and initiative training and resulted in an exercise that gave us our first sight of life outside the camp since our arrival.

Divided into teams of six, we were given an ordnance survey map with an objective to seek out, return and report back. We set off at 0900 hours each carrying a forty-pound backpack. It was a refreshing experience to be free from the harsh disciplines of camp life and we enjoyed every minute of it. Unbelievably, we set off marching in pairs. In such a short time we had become disciplined zombies, responsive to orders of command. When we realised we were 'free', we relaxed into a steady stroll. The sheer relief of the absence of Corporal Hawkins and the camp disciplines gave us an immediate lift. Instead of the conversation always revolving around camp issues, we were able to get to know one another. Our objective was a point on Caldy Beach, some ten miles south east of the camp. It was one of those rare bright, crisp and cloudless December days that sharpens the wits and makes you feel grateful for just being alive.

We located our map reference about midday and spent an hour relaxing on the beach at Caldy before starting our journey back. The map reading training had come up trumps, now all we had to do was 'live off the land'. We had been given no food and we hadn't a penny between us. We helped ourselves to a turnip a piece from a field we passed on the way back. We were well used to cattle fodder by this time and at least the turnips went some way to satisfying our craving for food and our parched throats. On our return even the mess food seemed more palatable.

Bull was the order of the day especially in the evenings. We spent hours ironing uniforms, polishing buttons and boots, especially boots. The new leather had a bubble finish that could be removed in various means. We used a spoon handle heated on the stove. The toe caps had to be honed to a mirror finish and to achieve it, a tin of black Kiwi polish, two dusters (one to apply the polish and the other to buff up), a strong index finger and plenty of spit were needed. The spit was applied to the polishing cloth then rubbed into the polish and thus on to the toecap in small circular movements. The boot was held between the knees and the folded duster did the rest. This was repeated dozens of times until a satisfactory shine was achieved. We knew that if it wasn't, we risked the boot of Corporal Hawkins scoring the surface and the whole process would have to be started from scratch.

Hawkins seemed to derive a sort of sadistic pleasure from seeing us squirm. One bitterly cold and freezing day in late December he kept us standing to attention, dressed only in our gym shorts, for almost one hour. A couple of the married boys complained to the officer in charge and suffered for it. When they returned to the billet, Hawkins ordered them to his room that was situated at the end of the hut. His voice could be heard all over the camp followed by furniture being knocked about and smashed. The boys' patience had run out and fisticuffs had taken over. Within a few minutes a ruffled Corporal Hawkins shot out of his room and returned with reinforcements. The two hatless airmen were double-quick marched across the square to headquarters where they were put on a 252 (charge form). The incident fizzled out after a couple days, but it gave us plenty to talk about at the time. Shortly after, it was discovered that Hawkins was in the habit of visiting the local pub on Saturday nights and staggering back to camp three parts cut. One night a few of the boys waited for him and returned some of his sadistic pleasure in kind.

All of us were selected for abuse at various times. My turn came on the parade ground, an area of the camp that was sacrosanct to all but authorised drilling. I cut the corner one day and was spotted by the ever-vigilant, hawk-eyed Hawkins. "Airman Titley, here, on the double!" he ordered. "Stand to attention when I'm talking to you!" He stood just a few inches away using his evil, eyeballing technique and his full vocabulary of expletives. I'd known that a situation like this was inevitable and had mentally prepared myself and rehearsed what I would do until I was word perfect. I stared at a spot on his forehead until he'd vented his spleen. He would have considered staring into his eyes an act of defiance. I amused myself by thinking of what a ridiculous spectacle he was making of himself; what his reaction would be if I told him and how his apoplectic display was doing more harm to him than it was to me. And there it ended. No charge, no extra duties, nothing. I even thought he had some atom of regard for me having cheered me on one day after a particularly hard session on the assault course.

A Staffordshire Lad

We were paired off and ordered to carry each other in turn on our backs for a distance of about eight hundred yards. My partner was an obese, fourteen stone, physical wreck who was gasping his last after only a few yards. I had to carry him practically all the way and we were first back.

On Sundays we had church parades and separated into our various denominations. These were the only occasions when we had any contact with the senior flight boys who were four weeks in advance of us. In spite of the ridicule experienced in other aspects of our training, there was no religious discrimination exercised. When the Blood Transfusion Service came on camp, diplomacy took over! "Stand at ease!" Corporal Hawkins ordered one day on the parade ground. "Those of you who have previously given blood, step forward!" A few of the older lads stepped forward. "Those of you who would like to volunteer, step forward!" The becoming more experienced junior flight had learnt never to volunteer for anything. No one stepped forward. "Step forward those of you who would prefer to give a pint of blood or spend four hours on fatigues!" He continued in this manner until he had more than half the flight willing to participate. Then he uttered a string of belittling taunts and humiliating comments to the remainder until he had the entire flight, other than those medically unfit, marching to the Blood Transfusion Service.

Fatigues were a way of life. Denims were issued for this specific purpose. Fatigues included all those tasks on camp that ordinarily the service would have to pay civilians to get done. They included stacking coke, peeling potatoes, cleaning offices and general duties. Each task was allocated with the organisation born of experience. No one managed to duck out of fatigues, although, experience taught us some short cuts.

A Staffordshire Lad

On Friday 24 December 1954, in spite of all the Hawkins' threats to the contrary, we were all issued with a form 295 (leave pass) and a travel warrant. The following day R.A.F. Transport ferried us to Lime Street station and from there we were on our own. Dad picked me up at Crewe station in his 1937 Morris Twelve, and half an hour later I was sitting in front of the fire sipping a real cup of tea, the first for over four weeks. It had been a long time since I had enjoyed the comfort of home as much as I did during that Christmas break in 1957. Joan and Ken were there, as was Mary and her fiancé Ken Johnson whom she was to marry in just ten weeks time. Granddad had provided his largest cockerel. Dad had made his biggest trifle and Mum was fussing about as if the prodigal son had returned.

I had been invited to a Christmas party at Phil Harrison's. All the old gang were there and, sadly it proved to be the last occasion when we would all be together. Brian Wright and Rags Riley were about to start their National Service in the Royal Navy; Marcia and Derek Rowley were going to teacher training college, Gwyneth Peirpoint was 'attached', and Malcolm Eardley was going to university to read Geology. No more were Malcolm and I to race each other across the gardens of the posh houses in New Road, leaping the hedges and fences like a couple of two year old steeplechasers. No more would we all compete in the cricket club's table tennis and billiards' tournaments. No more would we walk the lanes as carefree, happy-go-lucky school kids. We didn't realise it then, but it was the end of an era; the end of our happy teenage years together.

The Christmas holiday was soon over. My leave pass stated I must be back in camp by 0800 hours on Monday 28 December. My train left Crewe station at 0500 and I made it by the skin of my teeth. I'd slept in the armchair and had

A Staffordshire Lad

gone out like a light just a couple of hours before I was due to get up. Unusually, Dad had slept through the alarm. I disturbed at 4.00 am, woke Dad and we were on the road for 4.30. Never had that old tub gone so fast and never had my Dad taken such risks, but bless him, he got me to the station within minutes of the train leaving.

January meant more of the same, but we were now the senior flight and it was barely perceptible that we were treated just a little more leniently. We were allowed out of camp during the weekends. Occasionally we were given tickets to the local dances. One of these landed me into what could have been a nasty situation. I had been dancing with the girlfriend of the leader of the local pack of teddy boys and they were sharpening their razors by the exit when we were ready to leave. However, when they saw the size of my two minders, Jim Rowley and John Ryan they disappeared like mists in the night. We also went to the Grafton ballroom at Liverpool, later immortalised by the Beatles, but we didn't stay long. We took the friendly advice of one of the locals who told us that a military uniform was like a red rag to a bull in Liverpool and that we were asking for a lot of trouble if we stayed.

A squad of us were selected for funeral drill. Some military bigwig had died and we were to be the guard of honour. Funeral drill includes slow marching and a complicated range of moves with rifles resulting in inverting the rifle and resting the forehead on clasped hands over the butt. By the end of the week and after many hours of tortuous drilling on the parade ground, we came as near perfect as we were ever going to get only to find that our services weren't required.

During the first week of February we received our final test of 'reliability and initiative'. It had snowed quite heavily and proved to be the coldest snap since the winter of 1947.

We were issued with flying suits and leather jerkins and told to wear as many layers of clothing as we could get on. We were transported by lorry to the Snowdon range in Wales and dumped with all our kit at the side of the road. We had been divided into our teams of six. Each team had a tent and a primus stove. The food for each person for the three days' camp was three tins of bully beef and a packet of hard ship's biscuits. We had to lug the equipment three miles up the side of a mountain to the campsite and dig a foot of snow away to pitch the tent. The groundsheet was made up of individual waterproof capes buttoned together. It was pitch black. We had no lights and had to melt snow in our mess tins on the primus to make a cup of tea. We made one large bed with our blankets and snuggled down at about 2000 hours.

The following morning we were awakened at 0600 hours. As soon as it was light, we were given our objectives and map references with orders to report to the H.Q. tent as soon as we returned. The twenty miles' round trek took us over some of the most inhospitable terrain in North Wales, in sometimes blizzard conditions and at temperatures well below zero. We had to ensure that we kept closely grouped, well motivated and positive. We conferred regularly on our position and achieved our objective at midday arriving back at camp at 1600 hrs, just before dark. We had only eaten a couple of biscuits all day and were champing at the bit for our main course, the second tin of bully beef!

In spite of the adverse conditions, morale was pretty high and we spent most of the evening exchanging stories of our favourite meals. We bedded down quite early and were awakened at midnight. One member of another team had not returned. He was eventually found in a local farmhouse suffering with appendicitis. He had to be taken down the mountainside to a waiting ambulance. On the third day we broke camp and loaded all our kit into the transport. Tired and hungry, but with an acute sense of achievement, we arrived back at West Kirby to something approaching a hero's welcome. Apparently we were the first intake to have undertaken this type of exercise and the extreme conditions just added to its success. We had the best meal that the cook assistants had ever prepared followed by a steaming hot bath and an evening to share and reflect on our recent experience.

During our last week at West Kirby we were informed of our postings. It was the worst day of my life. Ten of us were told that we were being sent to Germany as Equipment Clerks! No appeal! No redress! Not even an opportunity to discuss the issue. Gone were my ambitions to fly, or to even work on the planes. I was devastated. From that day I lost all interest in the R.A.F. as a career and started to serve out my time. Later the ten of us discussed the reasons and the choice. The only common denominator was that we had all had a grammar school education and had achieved similar grades in our GCE's.

The sixth of February was our last day at West Kirby. We were given our passes, travel warrants and instructions of when and where to report. We packed our kit bags and spent the rest of the morning preparing for the afternoon passing out parade. In just eight weeks we'd been converted from a bunch of slovenly rag taggle gypsies to a smart, disciplined outfit. Mum, Dad and Aunty Ruth came to see the parade. The R.A.F. band played the march past and we were put through all the drill disciplines.

It was a day of mixed emotions. Thirty young men from diverse backgrounds had been thrown together for just a few weeks into a hostile environment of personal humiliation and crude, belittling taunts. The only relief we'd had was our mutual support, the solidarity for each other, the human warmth and the extraordinary comradeship. Many of us would never meet again. We were sad at parting, relieved to be leaving and happy to be going home. It had been an unforgettable experience. A time in my life that I would never like to repeat, and a time that showed the best and sometimes the worst sides of human nature.

I had some leave to reflect on my future. I was locked into the R.A.F. for the next three years. I decided to make the most of it and to get as much out of it as I could. At least I was going abroad at the taxpayers' expense.

My ten days' embarkation leave went quickly in spite of the utter feeling of loneliness. I was fitter and leaner than I'd ever been in my life and as straight as a ramrod. I was unused to the idleness and sedentary life at home. My pals were all at college, or work, or like me, doing their National Service. I missed the companionship of the billet and I had an inexplicable eagerness to be away from home.

As I previously explained, towards the end of the week I rang Uncle Harry and asked if I could spend the weekend with him.

• 4 •

After that memorable couple of days with Uncle Harry, and saying goodbye to him on the platform at Birmingham station, I travelled to Number Five P.D.U. (Personnel Despatch Unit) R.A.F. Innsworth, near Gloucester, one of the main transit camps for the despatch, receipt and demobilisation of R.A.F. personnel to and from abroad. Although Germany was considered a home posting, Innsworth was still used to process people either embarking on, or completing a posting with the Second Tactical Air Force. I met up with Jock Pugh and a few of the other ex-West Kirby lads and we had a pleasant and relaxing week interspersed with minor interruptions from various admin' orderlies responsible for our smooth transition to Germany.

We left Innsworth early on Sunday morning and travelled by rail across country to London's Liverpool Street station and then on to Harwich on the east coast. Eventually we were herded into the bowels of one of the services' three North Sea troop ships, the 'Empire Wansbeck'. The other two were the 'Empire Parkstone' and the 'Vienna'. The 'Empire Wansbeck' had been converted from a Second World War minelayer called the 'Linz'. In 1962, at the end of National Service, she became a Greek cruise liner, the 'Esperos'. Finally, she was 'blown up' by the Danish underground in the BBC series 'S.O.E'.

This was my first experience aboard ship and I was not impressed. The lower decks were allocated to the lowest form of service life. As well as R.A.F. personnel, it seemed to me that every regiment in the British Army was represented there. The canvas bunks were in three tiers and spaced about eighteen inches apart. I managed to get a top bunk thus avoiding the risk of having my head trodden on by the sweaty feet of those climbing up or down to the other bunks. The troop decks were uncomfortable, airless, hot and claustrophobic, and we were confined in these conditions until the ship was under way, normally about two hours. After this we were free to go to the N.A.A.F.I., or the open deck dependant on weather conditions.

• 5 •

The North Sea is notoriously rough, but my first crossing was relatively smooth. We docked at the Hook of Holland on Monday 24 February, just six hours after leaving Harwich. Civilian passengers, officers and their ladies, senior N.C.O.'s and their wives and then the rest left in that order. This was my first introduction to the class distinction that was rife in the services in those days. Once disembarked, we were ushered to a massive transit area and were given a good breakfast. I particularly remember the crusty white rolls so superior to the bread we had in Blighty. Then we had our sterling converted to Baffs, the currency used for the armed forces serving in Germany. With the exception of copper, there were notes for all denominations. Finally we were taken to the trains, massive in comparison to ours, and immaculate. Scores of Dutch cleaners were busy cleaning both the inside and outside. The trains were colour coded, green, red and blue, so as to identify destinations. The journey took us through Northern Holland passing famous towns like Utrecht and Arnhem.

There had been a heavy fall of snow and the Dutch children were enjoying the fun just as I had done at their age. It was different and I was thrilled by the differences. Surprisingly we were served a four course lunch on white tablecloths by white-coated waiters. Perhaps things were not going to be so bad after all.

We finally stopped at Buckeberg, a small town in Northern Germany. The castle was used as a transit camp and I remember it for two specific reasons. To me, on that night, it was the coldest place on earth, and it was the most inhospitable, formidable and scariest building I've ever had the misfortune to spend the night in.

The next morning I said goodbye to Jock Pugh who had been posted to a camp close by. I discovered that I was scheduled to go to R.A.F. Wahn near Cologne. From Buckeberg I travelled on my own and rarely have I been so excited with a journey abroad. I was so aware of the different smells,

A Staffordshire Lad

sounds and sights that as I write, almost fifty years on, I can still see and smell and hear them as if it was only yesterday. I am so blessed to have the ability to conjure scenes and situations of long ago that have been triggered by a familiar sound or smell. Over the years I have developed my senses so that I can absorb what they tell me. It is so sad that many of us look but do not see, hear but do not listen, touch but do not feel and speak without pre-thought or consideration. The heavy snow created scenes like Christmas cards and the familiar names brought to life the wartime stories I'd read. Krefeld then Dusseldorf and finally Cologne.

R.A.F. Wahn was equidistant between the major cities of Bonn and Cologne and served both as an airport. The Luftwaffe had developed the base in the thirties. In 1950 it was one of the 2nd. T.A.F's frontline bases, together with Celle, Fassberg, Gutersloh and Wunstorf. Back-up bases were west of the Rhine at Wildenrath, Geilenkirchen, Bruggen and Laarbruck. The 2nd. T.A.F. had a frontline strength of sixteen squadrons in 1950 and was equipped with Vampires and Meteors. These were later replaced first with Venoms and Sabres and by 1956, Hunters and Javelins increasing the strength to twenty-five squadrons. R.A.F. Wahn played host to Group Headquarters and to American and Belgian squadrons. There was also a detachment of the Royal Corps of Signals.

• 7 •

I arrived at the base feeling tired and a little bemused by the size of it. I reported in to the snowdrops at the guardroom. The duty airman took me to the billet where I was issued with blankets, bed linen and three 'biscuits' for my 'pit'. The billet was a two-storey block divided into rooms for two to six personnel. The standard of the accommodation was impressive with double-glazing, central heating and showers, baths and toilets on each floor. I was shown to my room. There was no one in, but three of the four bed spaces were occupied. I unpacked my kit bag, made my bed and lay there gathering my thoughts. I had arrived at the place that was to be my home for the next two and half years. The bed was the only piece of furniture on which to relax. There was a wardrobe and locker allocated to each bed space. When the other occupants arrived I sensed a reluctance to accept me; I was invading their inner temple, their most sacred few square feet. One of the boys told me to pick up my mug and irons and go with him to the canteen. I had been introduced to Nev Gartside.

Nev was tall and lean with black unruly hair untamed by Brylcream, piercing blue eyes and a deep, broad Yorkshire brogue that seemed to ooze out of the corner of his mouth. I liked him immediately. He proved to be honest, trustworthy, reliable and intelligent. He had a dry sense of humour expressed in a sort of disdainful manner, but without malice. To me, he came to personify the reluctant national service type with a uniform to match. He did the very minimum to stay within the rules. He looked like a refugee from Oxfam - his very appearance was an act of defiance. He'd only iron the front of his uniform for special parades. He brought to mind the verse from Rudyard Kipling's Gunga Din:

"The uniform 'e wore was nothin' much before, an' rather less than 'arf o' that be'ind."

He had a quiet confidence born of experience and an acceptance of his lot to see it through with a minimum of interference from those with rank who tried to impose it. Yorkshire was carved through him like a stick of Blackpool rock. He came from Knaresborough and supported York

City with fervour and passion. He exalted the rare wins and suffered in silence the many disappointments. His favourite player was Arthur Bottom and Nev had his own, earthier label for him. He bought the Daily Mail to read the sport and do the Quick Crossword. He'd invite me to help him with a clue and while I was thinking about it, with a twinkle in his eye and a vestige of a wry smile at the corner of his mouth, he'd complete the entire crossword having already worked out the answers in his head. Nev introduced me to everything, showed me everything and with his economical use of words, explained everything that I needed to know both at work and in our leisure time, and I mopped it all up like a piece of blotting paper. The other two roommates were a Brummy, Ted Insull and Derek Horsefield another Yorkshire man. Later we were joined by Dinger Bell. Changes were inevitably created with postings and demobs, and, as there were no restrictions on changing rooms, there was general movement and adjustment as new friendships were forged and old ones fizzled out.

On Monday morning I was introduced to my work as an equipment accounts clerk in E.P.A.S. (Equipment, Provisions, Accounting and Supply). The senior officer was Flight Lieutenant Palmer, who had come through the ranks in Transport Wing. He was a bit of a stuffed shirt, a solemn figure of pompous pretentiousness - full of his own importance. He took to the extreme that 'officers must not fraternise with the lower ranks'. He meted out discipline like a talking rulebook. Even though he'd been commissioned late in life, his pumped-up pomposity clearly demonstrated that he felt he'd been born to be an officer. Reporting to him was Sergeant Owen, known to us all as String; a thin, sallow complexioned and emaciated man from southeast London. He gave the impression that he'd just been lifted off a clothes peg. He wasn't such a bad bloke, but he had the infuriating habit of telling you what he'd done in the war. One day he said in his almost inaudible cockney brogue, "Did I ever tell you about the time I came face to face with six Japs in the Malayan jungle?" Nev said "No, but tell us how you manage still to be here."

The rules were read out to me and I was allocated half a dozen ledgers, a desk and a chair next to Nev who was to become my guide and mentor for the next few weeks.

The ledgers listed the stock of every single item stored on the camp. I had responsibility for aircraft components and the minimum storage was indicated in red against each component. Dropping below this level brought the wrath of God down on the offender's shoulders as it risked grounding an aircraft, an important strategic link in the chain of the 2 T.A.F's frontline defence. The system was quite simple. A stores demand note was issued for every item of equipment. The originals ended up in our office. The quantities were deducted from the ledger and, at a certain level, fresh stocks were ordered from the M.U's (Maintenance Units) in the UK. That was it. My boyhood dreams were shattered. The closest I was to come to an aircraft was a nut and bolt on a stores demand note. I made a couple of futile attempts to transfer to a trade without success. It was a sad indictment on the service in those days that it missed the opportunity to tap into its human resource, develop the skills and prepare for the inevitability of R.A.F. life after National Service. Consequently, I joined the ranks of the disinterested, merely going through the paces of daily routine, cherishing each leave and, ultimately, ticking off the days on my demob chart like everyone else. But there were also enjoyable times.

• 8 •

About fifteen of us worked in the office and three of these were Germans G.S.O's (German Service Operatives). The G.S.O's were mainly displaced persons resulting from the war and worked as part of a support organisation for the services in Germany. They carried out a variety of tasks including airfield guard. I became friendly with one named Norbert Nadler, affectionately known as Nobby. He was younger and more popular than the others and typified the Aryan with blonde hair, blue eyes and a good physique. He was engaged to the Commanding Officer's secretary, Marianne, a German woman who had spent some time in London before the war. Another, Heinz Parduhn was universally disliked. He was a carbon copy of the typical Hollywood Nazi. The third German was Bert. I could neither pronounce nor spell his surname. He spoke perfect cockney without a trace of accent. He'd learned to speak the language from the boys in the office.

Singing relieved the mindless work and tedium. All day long we'd join in chorus singing the latest songs as well as the old favourites. When we sang the old wartime songs the Germans joined in too. At 10.00 in the morning and 15.00 in the afternoon, the sound of the NAAFI van horn created a stampede, a clear indication of the interest we had in our work and the quality of the canteen food. Each morning before work, at lunchtime and after work we'd make our way unenthusiastically to the canteen in the futile hope that there might be some improvement on the usual tripe. The food was tasteless and boring, prepared without imagination and delivered with contempt. Next to the poor pay, it was the major gripe and the main topic of conversation. Occasionally a fleet-footed duty officer would appear at the canteen entrance with "Any" and disappear through the exit with "complaints?" Toad-in-the-hole was not only the speciality, it was our staple diet, and regularly served up for all three meals, sometimes with baked beans and other times with baked beans! Most of our paltry pay was spent on food at the NAAFI, Malcolm club and the local 'beirhausen'. Canteen food was a source of universal complaint. A letter written by some of the boys was printed in the Daily Mirror resulting in a high level visit of members of parliament. The quality of the food improved dramatically for the duration of the visit and afterwards resorted to its previous poor standard.

Fire picket formed part of the induction. 'Fire picket' was the original misnomer. It was the most humiliating duty we had to perform. For an agonisingly long week the Duty Fire picket had to report to the guardroom immediately after work and become the snowdrops' lackey; the official errand boy, until start of work the following morning. Snatches of sleep were taken on the hard board bunks in the cells at the back of the guardroom. It was one of the duties that was 'sold'. There was always someone willing to earn a few bob.

Hangar guard was another unwelcome interference into our leisure time and involved two two-hour shifts with a four-hour break for sleep. The sleeping area was a small room with a dozen or so biscuits on the floor. It was a depressing hole that smelled of stale air, rotten feet and body odour. The duty involved checking all the hangar doors and external equipment. Nights could be lonely and long, but it was fun scaring the GSO guards by operating the bolt on my rifle. They weren't aware that we had no ammunition and would shout out " guten abent, gay ess oh, gay ess oh"! I found a couple of places to get my head down when there was no risk of patrolling snowdrops. My favourite spot was in the A.O.C.'s (Air Officer Commanding) Avro Anson until it crashed in 1956 killing all on board. Another cosy spot d, and discovered much later, was the mortuary! The two benefits of hangar guard were that I could watch the night flying squadrons taking off to patrol the 'iron curtain' and also a 'flying duties' breakfast – bacon and two eggs.

The third duty was for EPAS personnel only. A term of 'Duty Storeman' lasted for one week and involved the receipt and unloading of vehicles arriving through the night, and the refuelling of transport. The 'bowsers' used for refuelling aircraft filled up with Avgas, high-octane aviation petrol, Avtur, aviation turbine fuel and Avtag, aviation turbine gasoline. Heavy transport used diesel and small vehicles, petrol. The duty storemen had a rest room adjacent to the offices that was almost respectable with beds, furniture and radio.

In those first few weeks it was impossible to come to terms with the sheer size and nature of the camp. There was constant air activity from the three all-weather night flying resident squadrons numbers 2, 68 and 87, and the civil flights including PAA (Pan American Airways), BEA (British European Airways), Sabena (Belgian National Airways) and Lufthansa (German National Airways). As well as the technical and administrative airmen and airwomen, there was a large squadron of the R.A.F. Regiment, the Rock Apes, whose main role was the defence of the airfield and equipment; a detachment of the Royal Corps of Signals; the GSO; 83 Group Headquarters and civilians who managed the leisure facilities. The Women's Voluntary Service ran the Malcolm Club, an establishment that welcomed all ranks of the service.

• 9 •

Our leisure time included regular visits to the camp cinema, which also provided live stage performances. The La Scala

Milan Opera Company tried out their latest production of 'Rigoletto' on us; we were 'experimented with' by the London show 'Salad Days'; Vera Lynn sang all the old wartime songs and how we loved and cheered her performance. We couldn't get tickets, but the cinema manager let us stand at the back. The British Forces Network (BFN) founded in 1942 and based in Cologne, put on talent shows that were broadcast live.

The wireless was our main link with home and Sundays, in particular, were special. We'd lie on our beds listening to 'Two Way Family Favourites' presented by Jean Metcalfe, the wife of the BBC broadcaster Cliff Michelmore. The programme was linked to BFN and requests were made from both ends. The Billy Cotton Band Show followed with Bill's 'Wakey, wakey' always opening the show.

But it was the extraordinary comradeship that helped us through the eternal drudgery and confinement. The NAAFI was the alternative to the barrack block. It provided quality food by comparison to the mess; a radiogram with a large selection of records; a bar and lounge; a shop that sold all the common necessaries; facilities for writing letters; comfortable furniture to relax on, and it was here that we would gather to air our grievances, share our confidences, argue our political and religious beliefs and generally put the world to right. There was a large register in the lounge where everyone was invited to fill in personal details and home addresses, and it was not unusual to be looked up by fellow locals who wanted to chat about things back home.

Whilst the NAAFI was for erks, the Malcolm Club was open to all ranks. It was more basic, yet more comfortable. It was here that we held our demob parties. We'd push all our tables and chairs together to form a great circle and everyone was encouraged to sing their favourite songs with all the rest joining in to sing the chorus, interspersed with the inevitable breaks to refill the glasses. And there was a great deal of talent. Derek Evans was a professional pianist. Eddie Loftus was a clever impersonator from the north east. He used to mime as a rolling drunk to Spike Jones' record "I went to your wedding," and he was always selected for the BFN talent shows that went out live on the BBC's Light programme. And there were many others who could entertain all night. We had one guy who would eat razor blades and light bulbs at the drop of a hat, and we had a chorus of very able singers. Although boozy, our demob parties were good entertainment guaranteed to launch the leaver into Civvie Street with a memorable bang, and to help the rest of us, for at least a few small hours, forget our moans and miseries.

Sport, also adequately provided for at R.A.F. Wahn, fired my adrenal glands and gave vent to my pent up energy. Inevitably, organisers and players of team games formed cliques resulting in the exclusion of those often more talented 'misfits'. Cricket was for officers and they went through a farcical 'diplomatic' process of team selection by eliminating other ranks using a variety of excuses. At one practice game, I was 'eliminated' for bowling out the captain.

The Wing had an abundance of boxing talent. We had a number of top-flight boxers including Ginger Leighton, the Second TAF champion. Boxing matches were very popular and well attended. Our heavyweight was Eric Henderson, a short-sighted, slightly punchy, good-natured scrap dealer from Nottingham. His somewhat half-baked attitude belied his intelligence and superb organising skills.

It was the informal practise and training sessions that were most enjoyable. Just kicking a football around and having a knockabout in the cricket nets tends to stick in my mind mostly. Occasionally in the summer evenings, I'd take

A Staffordshire Lad

Nobby Nadler to the athletics tracks for a work out. He was built like an athlete, but only built like an athlete! His sporting prowess was skiing and in winter, with his fiancée Marianne, he'd travel down to Bavaria at every opportunity. During the sunny Whitsuntide holiday in 1956, Roy Fox and I spent the entire four days taking turns to bat and bowl at each other in the nets.

Roy came to Wahn four weeks after me and we soon discovered that up to a point we had similar interests. He came from Stafford; we were the same age and had received a parallel education. He verged on the fanatical with regards to Wolverhampton Wanderers, Glenn Miller and James Stewart in that order. He also held extreme and radical views that led to disagreement and sometimes emotive argument. He became highly charged when an issue he believed in was strongly contested. Roy enjoyed alternative and zany humour like Stephen Potter and Tony Hancock, and later surrounded himself with sycophantic types from the same stable. These included Mick Jones, a Hancock look-a-like from Leeds, Ray Sharrock from Blackpool; Riva Jones who could stretch the truth to its extremity, so much so that his whoppers became standard jokes; Baz Holland, a Stretford boy whose entire vocabulary was Manchester United; Busby Babes; Duncan Edwards and Frank Swift. Roy inevitably latched on to Nev and adopted the same anti-establishment attitude. He became a father and a married man whilst at Wahn and, as a consequence, became more responsible. He is the only person with whom I remained in contact from my R.A.F. days.

The camp cinema was our means of escapism. Programmes changed two or three times each week and included all the latest films. We'd gather at the NAAFI for a drink and a bite to eat before making our way to the cinema. On one of these occasions, Roy and I were sitting at a table with Terry Fraser when someone accidentally bumped into my chair. It turned out to be Gerald Maddox, my former tennis partner from Audley. He joined us and to all our astonishment, had met Roy at Bethesda Street in Hanley when they'd had their medicals, and his girlfriend lived in the same Manchester street as Terry. It was just one of the many coincidences we experienced. I saw Gerald, who was in the Royal Corps of Signals, quite often afterwards.

Life outside of camp was mainly confined to a visit to the local beirhaus for a pork cutlet and a glass of lager. Occasionally we'd go to Cologne or Bonn by train. On the journey to Cologne the train inevitably stopped at the small station of Porz-am-Rhein just long enough for us to exchange our allocation of cigarettes into marks. In those days there were twelve marks to the pound and a carton of two hundred cigarettes that cost us a pound, could be sold for thirty marks. For those of us who didn't smoke, tobacco was our main currency. Cologne was still a city bearing the scars of war. The bridges in particular had been heavily shelled. Remarkably, the wonderful cathedral was relatively unscathed.

Once, we visited the world famous perfume manufacturers, 4711 Eau de Cologne, immortalising the city for perpetuity. Sometimes we'd travel to Koblenz, a beautiful town at the foot of the Drakensfels Mountains. The 1956 Easter holiday saw Roy, Ray, Riva, Baz and myself in the beautiful village of Rudesheim. We took our ground sheets and camped in a vineyard at the small suburb of Goddesberg. We later discovered that it was part of the estate belonging to Dr. Adenaur, the West German Chancellor. In the evenings we went to the village inn and sang songs for the locals.

The following Easter I went to Amsterdam with Derek Evans and David Wyles. We arrived in Amsterdam without a clue as to where we were going to stay. At the tourist information bureau we met two American girls who had already identified a guesthouse with rooms available, so we tagged along. The five of us had a few great days visiting the art museums, the Rembrandt gallery and birthplace, and perhaps the most enjoyable visit, the islands of Volendam and Mochendam where the locals continued to wear the traditional Dutch costumes.

Each year the GSO would arrange an annual outing. One of these included a visit to the great dams of the 'Dambusters' fame. The repairs to the gigantic holes caused by Barnes Wallis' bouncing bombs were still clearly visible. Another included a visit to Luxemburg and the inevitable wine tasting at a famous vineyard in the Moselle valley.

• 10 •

But it was our visits home that we looked forward to most eagerly. As regulars, we were given two lots of three weeks and a ten days continental leave each year with a three to four days' break for each of the bank holidays, and we took full advantage of them. I took my first three weeks' leave in July 1955. The journey turned out to be the worst I have ever experienced and the last time I travelled by land and sea until my demob.

We boarded the troopship Vienna at 8.00 p.m. Even in the shelter of the harbour a tremendous storm continually crashed the vessel against the quayside. Many of the hundreds of troops on board were seasick before the ship set sail. At midnight, with no sign of the storm abating, we were hauled out into the open sea by a couple of tugs and left to providence. The Vienna battled across the North Sea carrying its cargo of green-faced, vomiting human misery with it;

all fear of drowning driven away by the feeling of wanting to die anyway. The entire contents of peoples' stomachs rained down from upper to lower decks, from top to lower bunks. We were covered in it. We had to paddle through it. The only respite was to get to the higher decks for the cleaner air.

We docked at Harwich at midday. Twelve hours after leaving the Hook and six hours longer than the scheduled run. We were in a sorry state, but before our train arrived at Liverpool Street station we had restored some respectability. The first thing that struck me as we travelled through Suffolk was the astonishing greenness of the countryside.

My visits home formed into a general pattern. Weekdays I spent just mooching about in Newcastle and Hanley with an occasional visit to the cinema. Thursday afternoons, half-day holidays for those of my friends that worked in shops and banks, were the exception. Mostly I'd spend these with Brian Wright listening to his Nat King Cole records. Other than Brian, most of my former friends had left for college and National Service and it took me a little while to get used to Brian's new circle of pals. Keith Chesters and Phil Harrison had been part of our original group and I had known Ken Tarrant and Selwyn Booth from school. I had played tennis with Clive Rhodes, but Robert Lewis was new to me, as was Ken Clutton from Wood Lane.

Evenings were special with visits to the theatres and dance halls to hear our favourite bands like Ted Heath, Lonnie Donnegan, Johnny Dankworth and his wife Cleo Lane. At least once a week we'd play crib in the Boughey Arms at Audley and decide on our next excursion. Saturday nights inevitably meant a visit to Trentham ballroom calling en route at the Bull's Head, Hanford for a quick pint. When one of the big bands was playing at Trentham, all nine of us would pile into Robert's pre-war Ford twelve saloon, sometimes with a couple of girls in the boot.

Now and again we'd motor to Crewe town hall, Nantwich Civic, or as far as Buxton Spa ballroom to dance and see the top bands. On Saturday nights, after the dance, we'd call at one of our homes, fry a pan of chips and play records until the early hours. Once after leaving Robert's home, Brian and I saw a fantastic display of the Northern Lights. At four in the morning we spent half an hour explaining to the village bobby what it was all about. At odd times when friends were unavailable I'd go to the Majestic ballroom to polish up my steps. The dancing teachers were Eric and Carol Hand. Unfortunately, the ballroom was destroyed by fire in the 1960's. In those days I was relatively flush with money. We were always paid out in large white five-pound notes prior to going on leave and I was able to bring the boys lots of cigarettes.

Towards the end of 1955, Brian went into the Royal Navy for his National Service and I became more friendly with Clive Rhodes. He had recently completed two years in the Coldstream Guards and worked as a figure painter at Doulton's. He was a talented artist and a real ladies' man. No one had a chance with girls when he was around and occasionally he landed me in trouble with some of them. As we walked through the crowded ballrooms he'd pinch the girls' bottoms and I, following behind, got the stare or the slap and sometimes a surprised smile!

On sunny, summer Sunday evenings we'd walk across the fields to the White Lion at Barthomley, a distance of about four miles. And it was here that I disgraced myself. In spite of liking a drink, I have never been able to drink in quantity – a couple of pints have always been my limit. The White Lion was, and still is, a Burtonwood house. The beer suited not only my palette, but also my ticklish stomach, or so I thought. I was sober enough after my fourth pint to notice a few of the boys' raised eyebrows, and after my sixth pint they offered me a florin each if I could knock a seventh straight back. Never one to shirk a challenge, I drained the glass. My guts contorted and as my legs turned to jelly, Clive virtually picked me up and dragged me over the uneven floor to the gents. I was just conscious enough to notice the parents of an old school time girlfriend of mine staring at me with horror and some relief! I made it to the toilet just in time to see the entire contents of my stomach, seven pints and all, hit the porcelain. How I managed to walk the four miles back home is still a mystery to me. It wasn't funny at the time, but I've had many a smile about it since and I'm always reminded of the quote from "Modern Manners" by P J O'Rourke:

"Actually, there is no way of making vomiting courteous. You have to do the next best thing, which is to vomit in such a way that the story you tell about it later will be amusing".

On Sunday mornings we'd have a game of football with the local farmers at the back of the Rising Sun near Halmerend - 'Ommerend as it's known locally. There's nothing like a game of kick and rush and hair of the dog to see off early morning blues. The landlord of the Rising Sun knew this better than anyone and had up to twenty odd pints of shandy waiting for us on the bar after the game.

As well as the long leaves, I went home on most of the bank holiday breaks, always by air. Having the civil airport on camp was very convenient. Flying in the 1950's was still a luxury, but servicemen were allowed discounted rates. I could fly return from Wahn via London to Manchester for fifteen pounds. Aunty Ruth often ferried me to and from Manchester airport. She had a large pink and white Vauxhall Cresta, easily distinguishable from the air. On November

5th. 1956 I was flying to Manchester from Heathrow on a crystal clear night. As we dropped down over Staffordshire I could see the children's faces illuminated by the bonfires and I wondered if one of them might be at the old home in Cross Heath where I had enjoyed so many similar evenings in my childhood. One Saturday afternoon the plane's take off at Wahn was delayed to allow Winston Churchill's flight to land. He was visiting Germany to watch his horse run at the local racecourse. A massive guard of honour had turned out and the cheers were deafening when he gave his familiar victory salute.

The Christmas of 1955 was particularly memorable. Eric Henderson chartered our own plane. Thirty of us paid him twelve pounds each for the fare and we boarded the oldest DC 3 in the world, or so it seemed. We were loaded up to the gunnels with duty free drinks and cigarettes. Bottles of vodka were passed around to help us try and forget the sound of the coughing engines and general poor state of the crate. Just over the Channel, the port engine started to smoke and thankfully the pilot decided to land at Southend rather than risk the extra few miles to Heathrow. From Southend we were bussed into London and thereby made our respective ways home. The delay meant that I missed my connection at Stafford and had to wait for the milk train to Stoke that ultimately broke down at Barlaston with a further three-hour wait.

Stan Edwards, a former boyfriend of Mary's, and his fiancée were the only other people in the carriage. He was a regular in the army band and was one of the buglers that played the Last Post at the Cenotaph during the memorial service. The train finally arrived at Stoke station at 3.00 a.m. Mum and Dad had left an hour earlier thinking I wasn't coming so I had to walk with my suitcase the eight miles or so arriving home at 6.00 a.m. Three hours later I was with the boys, doing the circuit of all of our homes to wish everyone the best of the season and to share in their Christmas cheer!

The 1956 Christmas break was also in some doubt. The Suez Crisis resulted in all leave being cancelled and all services put on red alert. There was much activity to achieve a state of readiness and many of us were expecting to be shipped out to the Middle East.

There were a number of causes for the incident. Colonel Nasser, President of Egypt, wanted rid of the British base at Suez; he was jockeying for a United Arabia; he wanted to reduce the British and the French influence in the Middle East; the Eastern Block were supplying him with arms; the Russians were training his army; he had organised suicide bombers called Fedayeen, to cause mayhem in Israel, something that has a familiar ring to it nearly fifty years on; he blockaded the Gulf of Aqaba that leads to the Israeli port of Eilat and he nationalised the Suez canal.

With two thirds of British oil coming from the Middle East, Sir Anthony Eden, the new Conservative Prime Minister, with his French and Israeli allies decided to attack the airfields and land troops at Port Said on 29 October. With a presidential election looming, President Eisenhower declined to get involved and together with Russia and the rest of the world, condemned the British action resulting in a ceasefire on 6 November. It was a disaster for Britain and for Eden who, with his career in tatters, resigned in January 1957. Clearly, Eden and Eisenhower were as concerned about my leave as I was about their careers and with the hostilities at an end, all leave was restored and I made it home for Christmas once again.

At the end of my short break, I was waiting at The Pump all kitted up in full best dress uniform for the bus to take me to the station when I saw my Great Aunt Alice Dale across the lane beckoning to me. As always, she was dressed in black Victorian 'weeds', a straw bonnet and laced boots. She was petite and, although showing lines of care and wear, her face was appealing and her blue eyes bright and twinkling. She wished me luck, took my hand and pressed a florin into it; the widow's mite yet double the amount given to me by the Queen!

Ironically, as my service wore on, I found that towards the end of my leaves I was missing home. Not in Audley where I was having so much fun, but R.A.F. Wahn where I was so disinclined to be. This feeling has always puzzled me, but I suppose I had adjusted to a new way of life, I was maturing rapidly and my visits home were just opportunities for a change, much the same as holidays in working life.

• 11 •

Our only other contact with home was through letters. We avidly awaited the post, were excited when we received some and disappointed when we didn't. It was lifeblood to the married, engaged and courting boys and, inevitably there were those who received 'Dear John's', and who were consoled and cheered up in the usual ways. Sometimes we'd get a food parcel - another precedent for a party. Occasionally they had been opened by the military; a reminder that we were still at the height of the cold war.

Lying on top of my bed, the nearest thing to comfort we had, I became reflective. It was here I shared with myself those special memories of home, read my letters and planned for leaves and for the future. I thought of the bombing raids when I was a boy; how as a family we'd take refuge in the bathroom and drink cocoa. I wondered if any of those German planes had been based on this camp.

Mick Cady, Alan Bynon, and Colin Tingey replaced the departure of older friends such as Bill Campbell, Eric Henderson, and Corporal Chick Channon who had been my minder and confidante in the early days. The dynamic footballing talent of Jock Mearns and Jock Greenhoff also joined us. I finally shared a room with Johnny Kensett, a married man from Surrey, Ralph Hogg, a promising short story writer from Derby, David Wyles and John Wilson.

I became quite friendly with John Wilson. Before being called up he'd been a poultry farmer and we'd share stories and plan our future partnership in poultry farming. Sadly, John slipped on the ice and the glass pint pot he used for a mug cut through the tendons in his right hand. He was shipped back to Blighty for treatment and never came back to Germany.

Surprisingly, there were very few physical scuffles. As we were all in the same boat, we had learned to give and take. We helped one another. The smokers halved the last fag. We shared what we had and treated each other when the money ran out. However, if anyone slipped out of line, retribution was harsh. When one of the boys lacked personal hygiene and wet the bed after a night on the booze, he was stripped, thrown into the bath and scrubbed until he was clean.

Generally I got off lightly with most things, particularly when I was going on leave for the first time an over observant snowdrop noticed I'd slashed the peak on my cap. Chick Channon, the stores corporal, came to my rescue and saved me from certain discipline, or at least the cancellation of my leave. Stores personnel wielded a lot of power. They were responsible for replacement clothing and laundry. It was not unusual for someone, after upsetting a storeman, to receive badly soiled clothing back from the laundry, or wrong sized replacement clothing.

I was not so lucky when I was caught laughing on parade and was charged for 'guffawing'. The following day I was marched hatless, at the double between two NCOs and brought up in front of our Wing Commander, Squadron Leader Elshaw, a Second World War hero. I was given seven days 'jankers' (confined to barracks). This meant full inspection every evening after work and weekends at the guardroom, and menial tasks afterwards.

As demob became more than a glimmer of light at the end the tunnel, thoughts inevitably turned to Civvy Street and a career. I had illusions to become a teacher and, as a consequence, decided to improve my qualifications. In those days, the minimum qualifications for entry were five GCE's, so in order to improve my chances I took and passed English Language and took and failed 'A' level Geography. Squadron Leader Long, the Education Officer, arranged for me to take the Geography examination at Hohne, an army base in northern Germany. The exam was a stickler, but I enjoyed my visit. The food was good and I met Gary Nicholson my old classmate from Newcastle High. In the evening we went to see the former concentration camp of Belson that was a couple of miles from Hohne. I was awestruck by the sheer scale of the camp. Many of the giant pits where the remains of so many unfortunate souls were buried were clearly visible as were the empty ones left as a reminder to what could have been. The giant memorials told the story and I was amazed at how many Russians had died there. There was a secure route from East Germany, just a few miles away, where Eastern block relatives could visit the graves. We were told that the dignitaries and local people from Hohne, who had denied all knowledge of what had gone on at the camp, were transported there by the allies to see for themselves. On the way back we hitched a lift on a Jeep driven by a lunatic army sergeant. He took us over the tank testing ground. It is the most hair-raising white-knuckle ride I have ever experienced, but it did help us to put what we had just seen to the back of our minds.

I secured an interview with Alsager Teachers Training College and attended on my last leave. It was a lesson for the future. I was completely unprepared as to what to expect. Six very austere and venerable old men sitting on a platform and demanding to be looked up to, formed the interview panel. The questions were vague and sometimes subjective and, it seemed to me, designed to make me uncomfortable. If that was the case, it worked, resulting in a letter that informed me "I had been unsuccessful on this occasion, etc." From that moment I lost interest in teaching. Alsager was the only local teachers' training college and I had no desire to be away from home for another three years.

During the summer months of 1957 R.A.F. Wahn was being systematically handed back to the German Luftwaffe and on 18 July there was a formal parade and ceremony to exchange the flags. As equipment accounts clerks we were mainly involved in married quarters' audits, checking all 'items household' and draining the left behind, partly opened bottles from the cocktail cabinets! My corporal's tapes had come through at Easter time and Flight Lieutenant Palmer had tried to bribe me with them by extending my service to see the handover completed. I refused on the grounds that, at the time, I was hopeful of securing a place at college, so I remained S.A.C. (Senior Aircraftsman) until my demob.

• 12 •

And so the day arrived on 17th. August 1957, exactly two and a half years to the day after setting foot in Germany, my tour completed, I found myself leaving the place I'd come to know as home. Thankfully, I hadn't been given another posting because a three months period was considered too short to be economical. The previous night's party reached a successful conclusion; all the handshakes had been made; my bed space cleared away and my kitbag and suitcase packed. There were no feelings of sadness – just relief that it was all over, I'd survived and was on the threshold of a new life. The journey to the Hook was without incident, but who should I see in the canteen? Jock Pugh, exactly where I'd left him two and a half years ago. In fact, with the first class organisation and precision of the armed forces, I met a number of the boys that I'd been with on the outward journey.

We arrived once more at R.A.F. Innsworth, but this time for demob. The processing took three days. I declined the demob suit and took the money instead. I collected my certificate of discharge, outstanding pay and travel warrant, and on the 21 August 1957 became a civilian once more. I dragged my kitbag down the entire length of Diglake Street in an act of defiance.

Outwardly I hadn't changed a great deal, but inwardly I had become a different person. National service had released me from the steadying influence and demands of home. It had given me an independence not experienced by boys entangled in the network of domestic relationships and the constraints of teenage life. When too young to vote and old enough to serve, I had been thrown into a new world of young men of similar ages, experienced the extraordinary comradeship and developed the ability to eat, live and sleep with all types, from a variety of backgrounds and from every corner of these islands. As there were good times so there were bad ones, but these, with the salve of life, have been mellowed by the mists of time.

CHAPTER NINETEEN

RE-VISITING

I promised Ann before we were married that one day I would take her to see the location of the old camp in Germany. For a long time I contemplated how I should do this. This year, 2007, was the fiftieth anniversary of both the transfer of command of Wahn from the Royal Air Force to the German Luftwaffe, and of my demob, so it seemed an appropriate time to make the effort. After much research, and a letter to the German Embassy in London, I discovered that the camp was still in existence and that I was to be contacted by a senior officer in order to make arrangements for the visit. We decided to take a few days holiday in the Moselle valley using a day to travel up to Wahn.

On 20 November we travelled by train from Koblenz to Porz am Rhein, the small station where I used to convert my cigarette ration into German currency more than fifty years ago. The station has changed very little, but Porz has been converted from a country village into a thriving town. The growth of Cologne's suburbs has completely enveloped the

A Staffordshire Lad

area. In fact the only part that I recognised was the main street of Wahn leading up to the camp.

We were collected by Lieutenant Colonel Trares in a large chauffeur-driven car at the station. He was as perfect a gentleman as was his command of English. We were given a tour of the camp by car with the exception of the airfield and that, because of tight security, was strictly military staff only. I was overwhelmed by its size. Most of it was unrecognisable. Almost everything had changed other than the old barrack blocks now converted into offices.

We walked round a small military cemetery. The Colonel was amazed that I hadn't seen it before, and even more surprised to learn that this area that housed the officers' mess and open-air swimming pool was the preserve of officers only and out of bounds to all other ranks. The cemetery contained the graves of French and Belgian soldiers that had been killed within the precincts of the camp, and also two First World War German soldiers that had been shot for mutiny at the end of the war.

The highlight was a visit to the guard-room, the first and last place I saw of RAF Wahn. It has been converted into a museum and was opened especially for our visit. The rooms have been converted to house memorabilia from the two hundred years of the camp's history. The cell where I slept during my weeks of fire picket and jankers now houses the visitors' toilet; the hard bed is strapped to one of the walls. I was particularly interested in the camp's use during the Second World War and was surprised to learn that it was mainly kept as a reserve; a back-up bomber and fighter station. I was shown a photograph of the ceremonial parade when the camp was handed back to the Luftwaffe on the 18th July 1957 on which I attended, just six weeks before I was demobbed. One of the curators took me into the cellar to see if I could throw any light on a large notice that was kept there. It was a large sheet of metal about a quarter of an inch thick. It was the official sign for 83 Group Headquarters also based on the RAF camp. On the back were what appeared to be a German coat-of-arms and some gothic writing that translated into 'church garden'. I told them that it was likely that the sign had been stolen from a church to be used for the Group HQ sign.

We had our photographs taken signing the visitors' book and handing over the report that I had written covering my period at the camp.

I have a lasting impression of the warmth, friendliness and extraordinary welcome extended to us on the day. In spite of the fact that I hadn't recognised a great deal – I hadn't been prepared for so much change – it was a most enjoyable day and I had achieved a long-standing ambition and promise to my wife all those years ago.

Epilogue

I have always considered my childhood to be very ordinary. I was just a simple, run of the mill lad from an ordinary working class family growing up with kids who had similar backgrounds. The older I get the more grateful I become for the good fortune I had in being born in such an environment, surrounded by homely folk with good family values, impeccable standards and great humility. It is a lost time; the end of an era. A time of unlocked back doors; good neighbourliness; sharing; back kitchens; back yards; corner shops; orderly queues; running errands; family circles; make and mend; making do.

I had proved to myself that I had the ability, tenacity and perseverance to survive against the odds, and the personality and flexibility to get on with all kinds of people; particularly those of my own age and gender. I now had to prove that I could secure a career, stand on my own feet and contribute to society in the way young people were expected to do so in those days. It was an exciting prospect and resulted in providing me with a most challenging, fulfilling and extremely happy 'rest of my life'.

Those That Touched My Early Life

Until the age of sixteen, my friends had been those living within shouting distance from home with the exception of school pals. Brian Johnson remained a bachelor and, as far as I am aware, continues to live in the old family home in Orton Road. I had a telephone call from him in the 1970's when he'd found a letter I'd written to his mother after the death of his father. He said he would contact me again, but I've not heard from him since.

I have recently been reacquainted with Pat Washington, one of the kids from the Block. She lives just across the fields with her husband, Peter Bridden. He was in my year at Newcastle High, although we never knew each other. He must have been one of the clever ones!

I saw Graham Roberts to speak to only once when I was about eighteen and we sat together on the Mainwaring bus from Newcastle to Cross Heath. He became quite a local entrepreneur and I last saw him on television being interviewed regarding a dispute with the locals about a large open-air market he'd organised at Rayleigh Hall, Eccleshall. I think of him often and of the many happy times we shared together from our infancy to adolescence. I tried many times to get in touch with him without success until I remembered a cousin

A Staffordshire Lad

of his, John Moss, and after trawling through the telephone directory I spoke to John and he gave me Graham's telephone number. I called Graham and we spent a happy hour sharing a potted history of lives as well as recapturing some of those treasured times of our youth. He became a member of the Army motorcycle display team during his National Service. After demob, he bought a second-hand lorry, the first of a fleet that he eventually built up. It was a real pleasure to hear that he has made so much of his life. He has two children and two grandchildren and lives at Clayton with his wife Jean.

Brian Wright's death in his forties took me a long while to come to terms with. Although Peter Anderson and John Evason had died in their early twenties, Brian had been very close and we'd shared so many good times. It's nice to imagine him relaxing somewhere in the cosmos listening to Nat King Cole's silver tones.

Derek and Marcia Rowley became teachers, as did John 'Rags' Riley. John did his national service in the Royal Navy and was fortunate in serving in the ship that accompanied Sir John Hunt's expedition to the Antarctic in the late 1950's. Rags died in 2003.

Clive Rhodes married his school-time girlfriend Beryl Plant and became the local milkman in Miles Green and Audley. I haven't seen him or any of the others since 1958.

I have stayed in contact with Roy Fox until quite recently. He continues to live in Stafford. We worked for the same firm, starting and retiring at the same time. After our demob we had a reunion with Eric Henderson and David Wyles in Nottingham during November 1957. Eric became a successful Nottingham businessman dealing in waste metals. David visited me in 1959 prior to getting married. Ray Sharrock also called to see me when he was visiting Roy who at that time lived only a few doors away from me. Ray was a long distance lorry driver.

I went to see Nev after his demob and stayed with him for a weekend at his home in Knaresborough. I discovered through Roy that he'd become a rather portly solicitor in later life.

John Wilson looked me up a couple of times. Once in 1957 when I missed him after he called at Diglake Street and again in the late seventies when I was living at Stafford. After his demob he had difficulty in settling down and rejoined the R.A.F. at a time when computers were being introduced. His flair brought him rapid promotion and even then held the senior rank of squadron leader.

I have recently heard that Gerald Maddox is no longer with us, but this is not confirmed. I hope that it isn't true. Losing life's contacts chips away at the whole. The sound of the grim reaper becomes increasingly more audible. I feel it's time to draw a line under this narrative and preserve it in some way.

At various times throughout my life I have revisited the places where I grew up and on all those occasions I have never seen any of my old friends, no doubt they are all scattered to the four winds like the old verse:

Like mists that round a mountain grey
Hang for an hour then pass away.
So I and nearly all my race
Have vanished from my native place.
Each haunt of childhood's loves and dreams
More beautiful in fancy seems,
And if I to these scenes repair
I find I am a stranger there.

About the Author

Harry Titley was born in 1936 in a poor area of Newcastle-Under-Lyme in Staffordshire, the county where he has lived for most of his life and about which most of his story is told.

The youngest child of a working class couple, both from families with long histories in coal mining, he grew up during the Second World War where, in spite of lives being on hold, he had a childhood freedom that was not experienced by generations of children before or since. It is a time where so much has been lost and mainly forgotten. His sensitivity and his contentment with his lot helped to consign those times to memory, 'a thousand latent joys and half-forgotten sorrows'.

After completing his national service in Germany he went to work at the English Electric company in Stafford where he remained until his retirement in 1999. He married Ann in 1960 and they had one child, Julie, in 1961.

Although 'A Staffordshire Lad' is Harry's first book, he has written some poetry and a number of articles for a Canadian magazine and local newspapers. During his working life he was editor of the company-wide magazine. He now lives in the North Staffordshire countryside with his wife.

Lightning Source UK Ltd.
Milton Keynes UK
12 December 2009

147432UK00001B/73/P